a little bit of

angel
numbers

a little bit of

angel
numbers

an introduction to
messages from the universe

NOVALEE WILDER

STERLING ETHOS
New York

STERLING ETHOS
New York

STERLING ETHOS and the distinctive Sterling Ethos logo
are registered trademarks of Sterling Publishing Co., Inc.

Text © 2023 Novalee Wilder

ISBN 978-1-4549-5259-6
ISBN 978-1-4549-5260-2 (e-book)

For information about custom editions, special sales, and premium
purchases, please contact specialsales@unionsquareandco.com.

Printed in India

2 4 6 8 10 9 7 5 3 1

unionsquareandco.com

Cover and interior design by Melissa Farris
Cover and interior illustration by VectorSun58/Shutterstock.com

contents

INTRODUCTION

Are numbers following you around? Do you keep glancing at the clock at 11:11, do the numbers in your birthdate show up as the total on a receipt, or do you wake up at the same time each night? Maybe you notice the numbers on highways and bus routes or see patterns in phone numbers, bank statements, or house numbers over and over again? If so, you are not alone.

If you have ever felt that there was a meaning behind the numbers that kept eluding you, then this book will help you catch it. If you're scratching your head trying to make sense of why you see a specific number or sequence at the same time each day, use the book to look up the message behind it. In the coming chapters, we will look at why you're noticing numbers in ever-increasing ways and what they mean. We will look at your personal angel numbers, how to work with your angels on a deeper level, and what it means if you stop seeing the numbers. I will answer the most common questions about angel numbers as well.

I wrote this book for people like you, who are waking up to their own spirituality and starting to see all the ways the Divine is whispering through everyday occurrences, serendipitous moments, signs, and numbers. Not so long ago, I walked through the world not really noticing the details, the synchronicities, and the music of the Divine that echoes in all there is. It felt like I couldn't fully tune into the radio station that was broadcasting messages from my spirit guides. I would get words and intuitive nudges here and there, but each time I'd feel equal parts elated and confused. I had to learn to quiet my mind. How to become receptive to what was being revealed to me. How to realize that spiritual guidance cannot be controlled or received without a certain level of surrender. Further down my path to becoming a professional numerologist, I studied numerology for years through group training and with master teachers. As the system I'm trained in became a fully embodied experience, the numbers turned into another language for my intuition to use and my higher power to speak and provide support through. My wish for you is that the more you engage with the numbers and explore the pages ahead, the more you'll recognize and feel the comfort and support the angels are offering to you.

This book is not a full introduction to the field of numerology and the spiritual and practical study of the numbers, letters, and vibrations they hold. We will use the Chaldean numerology system as the foundation but will zoom in on the first thousand angel numbers and all the questions that can come up as you open up this channel of communication with your higher power.

When we develop our intuition and spiritual gifts, we see that the Divine and our guardian angels are always trying to help and support us. Yet we will very rarely get the full picture or long-term schedule delivered on a silver platter. Our angels prefer to send encouragement, gentle course corrections, affirmations, and/or clarification of a situation, relationship, or choice ahead of you. The messages are simple but provide a higher perspective. Even when our angels ask us to stop or slow down, it is with a gentle hand on our shoulder, never interfering with our free will.

You can use this book as a reference when you start seeing the numbers, and when you want to go deeper with any message you see repeatedly. I've also included a suggested list of prompts for beginning an angel numbers journal to track your progress and understanding over time.

NAMING YOUR HIGHER POWER

A note of how I approach naming the energy that the angel numbers represent: In this book, I will use words and phrases such as *your higher self, the Divine, angels, Universe, God,* and more. They will be used interchangeably, and you are free to use, ignore, or replace them with the words that resonate with you. You don't have to use any specific name or even be consistent in your naming of the energy that shows up to guide you. It could be God, Goddess, Creator, Divine, Source, Gaia, Universe, your higher self, big U, She-who-is-all, the angels, spirit, ancestors, or the name of a specific deity or saint. Use the words and names that feel right to you in the moment. You'll find that specific clues and aspects of a message are revealed through the context, language, and words you chose to describe and name the power behind it.

WHAT IS NEEDED FROM YOU TO USE THIS BOOK

The language of angel numbers and the messages behind them are not a closely guarded secret reserved for only a select few. There is no judgment or punishment for not engaging and no timeline or end goal that you need to meet. A pure intention of wanting to connect and communicate with your angels is the only thing you need to start a conversation with the Divine.

The numbers are almost always a "go" sign, signifying that you're being invited to play and engage with the energy offered. There are very rarely any negative messages or connotations to the numbers. If you feel fear or aversion around a message or learning more, this is a sign that you need to slow down, ground yourself, and allow your higher power to clarify it for you. We can be as afraid of expansion as we are of rejection. If you have a negative perception of your own spirituality, then healing could be needed for you to allow the angels to be a source of support and encourage-ment going forward.

If you would like some extra support on your journey, I've created a meditation to deepen your connection and sharpen your focus when communicating with the angels. I also created a playlist while writing this book to accompany your reading. You can find them through the link at the end of this book (see page 109).

1

what are angel numbers?

Before we get to the number part of this book, we first have to look at the messenger behind the message. In almost every religion, counting both ones that center around one deity and ones with a pantheon of gods and goddesses, the concept of angels as messengers of Divine will is present. While the depiction of their power, features, area of influence, and motivation varies a bit within each belief system, the most unifying trait of angels is their desire to protect, guide, and encourage spiritual growth in their charges.

In the Vedas, the earliest literature of Hinduism, the guardian angel is seen as a type of deity in and of itself comprised of two separate but similar forces: Devas and the Atman. Devas are gods in their own right, but can also act as angels as they guard, support, inspire, and fuel the spiritual evolution of all living things. The Atman is the unique sacred spark of divinity within each of us. Our eternal higher selves are always seeking to strengthen the connection between our human selves and higher levels of consciousness. Together the Devas and the Atman inside of you are working on becoming one with the Divine.

THE LANGUAGES OF THE DIVINE

Angel numbers are one of the languages the angels use to communicate with us. The angels can both speak for and connect you to your ancestors, all aspects of the Divine, and any spiritual messenger that is part of your spiritual support team at this moment in time. During our life, we have a core team of angels and spiritual guides who are always there. At times we get extra attention, specialized support, or visits from deities that might not be part of our upbringing, religion, or previous spiritual understanding. Our personal guide team is filled with supporting energies that reflect where we've been, what we need right now, and what is coming up in our near future.

You might be well versed in the realm of angels and in an ongoing conversation with your own spiritual team. Or you might at times just have felt a point inside you stretch toward a bigger point or loving presence outside or even deeper inside yourself. No one alive on earth has been without angelic encouragement, but the vast majority of us have not paid attention to it or pursued a conversation with the angels.

Beyond the reading of this book, you could feel called to learn more about angels through religious and spiritual scripture. You might be comforted by knowing that a benevolent force is on your team and over time start to be able to energetically differentiate between the messages from separate aspects of your angelic team. From the everyday occurrences to the mystical, serendipitous, and magical moments where the sense that something greater is speaking to you, you will feel the presence of the Divine at your back.

ANGEL NUMBERS AS MESSAGES FROM THE UNIVERSE

Angel numbers are single digits, compound numbers, and number sequences that may appear in ordinary settings and can be interpreted as messages from a higher power or your spirit team. They can provide insight into complicated situations and shed light on themes you currently are experiencing in your life. They can show up as single digits, repeating number sequences, or ascending or descending numeric cycles. They can appear as numbers you already know, like your birthdate, phone number, or license plate, or even in the form of seeing other signs a specific number of times. You could go through the procession of seeing the number 333, then encounter other signs in groups of 3, notice house numbers that have a digit sum of 3, and end with seeing 3 feathers every day on your way to work for a while—until the energy shifts. You could also see numbers when you're in a particularly relaxed and receptive mood while watching TV and notice apartment, hotel room, or street numbers in your favorite TV series.

Angel numbers can show up as a message, confirmation, or reminder. They can offer you an affirmation to help you shift your focus or anchor your ambitions in a new goal. They are often like flashes of light that lead you down a path to deeper spiritual experiences and connections. When the meaning of an angel number is phrased as an affirmation, it might be prudent to shift your thinking to a more positive outlook than the one you currently have.

WHY WE SEE ANGEL NUMBERS

The numbers appear when we are starting to open up to help and support from the Divine. The messages come through when we need them, whether it be at the start of a journey, before a big decision, when we level up in some way in life, or around big transitions in general.

Noticing what your mind is occupied with when you see them can show you why you're specifically seeing them.

HOW TO CONNECT WITH YOUR ANGELS

The beginning of any deeper connection starts with an intention to open to it. By stating your desire to work more closely with your angels, you give them permission to appear more readily and communicate more intimately with you. If you have already set the intention, the next step is to allow yourself to listen to the language that your angels most easily use to deliver their support and messages.

THE HISTORY OF ANGEL NUMBERS

Until just before the turn of the 21st century, angel numbers were most often referred to as "divine numbers" or "spiritual number sequences" and had yet to get their own, widely used designation within the field of numerology. That changed when the author Doreen Virtue wrote a series of books about angels and angel numbers in the late 1990s and early 2000s. Through Virtue's books, the terminology and use of angel numbers entered the global consciousness in a way that has only intensified over the years. Like many other esoteric and spiritual tools, they have become mainstream in the same vein as astrology and the tarot.

Before Virtue wrote her books, most people who worked with the esoteric aspects of numbers only looked at them through the lens of the numerology system they were most familiar with. This is why, depending on the background and schooling of the numerologist you ask, you'll hear different takes on the numbers. On top of that, the meaning and message behind angel numbers have always been much more open to personal interpretation than most other spiritual tools.

2

repeating angel numbers

All numbers have general meanings, messages, affirmations, and areas of life that they speak to. You might pick up on the universal message behind the patterns you see and still need more information to clarify an experience or correlation. As you work with the numbers, my recommendation is to sit with the single digits and sequences you see and journal about what comes up. If journaling does not work for you, try recording an audio message for yourself where you talk through the emotions and thoughts present in this moment. Just as journal entries can help us track patterns over time, listening back to audio messages makes us remember the exact energy present.

Repeating numbers hold the energy of the single number within them in exponentially increasing ways and are some of the most noticed number sequences.

0: 00, 000, 0000

0s speak of potential and the moment before inception. This is the gathering of power before a beginning, leap, change, or creation. 0 is also the number of the pause. It holds vast expanses of possibility. Most people miss these sequences when they show up as they are subtler than the subsequent ones. Seeing 0000, known as the "Gates of Potential," is a sign that energetic doors are opening, that any move you make now could impact the rest of the journey profoundly and that the angels are waiting to support your next action.

1: 11, 111, 1111

The number 1 is about creation, new beginnings, and a focus on yourself. Repeating 1s are a reminder to pay attention to what is starting to happen, the nudges you get to explore something new, and to keep going with what you want to create. Seeing repeating 1s is an indicator that you're ready to respond and engage with the world. No need to hide or wait. Go share, teach, and pass on your knowledge now. Trust your intuition. Seeing 1111, known as the "Gates of Light," is a sign that you're one with your path, that the sacred mechanics of the Universe are turning the wheel of fate in your favor.

2: 22, 222, 2222

The number 2 is always revealing layers of and pointing to relationships and heart connections. It teaches us about giving and receiving in equal measure. The focus of the 2 is on your relationships. Seeing lots of 2s tells you to have fun and let go. Don't overthink or plan your next steps too much; look for an invitation instead. Seeing repeating 2s is an indicator to look for balance with regard to how we take care of others and let others take care of us. Be open to help and support from the world. Seeing 2222, known as the "Gates of Patience," is a sign that you're being lifted and guided by the angels. No matter what heartache or loss of connection is in your past, new loving relationships and allies are coming your way.

3: 33, 333, 3333

The number 3 draws our focus to work, ambition, and luck. Noticing 3s tells you to own your goals and expertise, to step through the door from student to master. If you believed you had luck on your side and could not fail, what would you do? Seeing 3333, known as the "Gates of Luck," is a sign that things are aligned for a big leap, a stroke of luck, or a serendipitous opportunity. The questions here are: Why not you? Why not now? When destiny comes knocking, please open the door. Let the angels of luck and opportunity show you how good it can be.

4: 44, 444, 4444

The number 4 speaks of change and transformation. It wants you to trust that you can expand into new or different levels of life, but also that you might need to move or change something drastically to do so. Repeating 4s point to a rebirth and foundational work in your life. This could also be about structures and core beliefs that need reimagining or reinforcement. 444 and seeing repeating 4s are signs that you signed up for this particular challenge; you have what it takes and will make it through. Seeing 4444, also known as the "Gates of Change," is a sign to focus on your support systems, build a foundation, and trust the ride. You have asked for change, and, as you step into the path of transformation, you become a messenger of hope for others who are wanting to make big shifts too.

5: 55, 555, 5555

The number 5 is always in flow, focused on continuous movement and energy. Seeing 5s means that inspiration and value are coming through other people and your connection with them, however fleeting. 5 is connected to any exchange of energy, finances, messages coming from far away, and both international and local travels. Seeing 5s coincides with the angels speaking through conversations around you, snippets of music, or the sense that you're eavesdropping on messages from the cosmos. Seeing 5555, known as the "Gates of Connection," implores you to say yes to the invitations of your network and connections. Those answers and information can come from literally anywhere, and the only limits of receiving them lie in your capacity to open the doors for the angels to bring you closer to the people, places, and abundance that are already on their way to you.

6: 66, 666, 6666

The number 6 speaks about love on the deepest level. This could be the angels pointing you to family or close relationships, to the awareness that your ancestors are in the wings waiting to help, or to the understanding that you might need extra protection and guidance in the near future. 6s can show up when loved ones pass over or when a new soul is ready to be born. Repeating 6s are an invitation to explore and enjoy everything in your human experience and all of the physical, emotional, and spiritual aspects of your life. Seeing 6666, also known as the "Gates of Love," is a sign that love is the strongest force in your life right now and to listen to your heart. Stepping through this gate is letting the angels help you dissolve everything that blocks you from realizing that we are all one, intrinsically connected and dependent on each other.

7: 77, 777, 7777

The number 7 speaks and points to messages from our higher self or soul. It's one of the most spiritual numbers, and it reminds us that everything is possible through faith. When 7s show up the veil is thin, and you should make time to daydream, meditate, doodle, and just spend as much time being open to inspiration as possible. 7 is known as the "phone number to heaven," so when 7s show up, you need to be ready to answer the call. Seeing 7777, also known as the "Gates of Intuition," means that the angels have a task of creation for you. You can now call on the muses of all creation, and through you, new ideas and worlds can be born and merge into this one. As you connect with your higher self and the aspects of you that are connected to the angelic realms, you lift the vibration of everyone around you and in your lineage.

8: 88, 888, 8888

The number 8 speaks of predestined things or karmic lessons and authenticity. Seeing lots of 8s means it is time to be bold and to strike. There is nowhere to hide if lots of 8s show up, so you might as well own your choices and speak your mind. Seeing repeating 8s points to a lesson of balance, responsibility, and abundance. We're either in almost perfect balance or not able to let go of the responsibilities that drag us off course and aren't ours to deal with. The angels want you to be clear in your choices. Take inventory of where you step up when you should be stepping aside. Seeing 8888, also known as the "Gates of Karma," is a sign that it is time to break old patterns. The choices you make now will free or change things for all the people connected to you and for the generations before you.

9: 99, 999, 9999

The number 9 takes us to the finish line. The theme that shows up is about completion and resolving issues that hold us back from letting things go. Seeing 9s means that the angels want you to look at your actions when it comes to boundaries, anger, temptation, and material things. 9s signify endings, and sometimes that means you will be woken up to some harsh truth or injustice. Like with the number 6, 9 can show up when loved ones pass over or when a new soul is ready to be born. Seeing lots of 9s means that you're ready to let go. It could be releasing a physical reality, a past belief, or a way you have kept yourself small. The angels are teaching you to see the world objectively and detach from old reactivity. Seeing 9999, known as the "Gates of Completion," means that a cycle is ending, and it's time to let go of old baggage and to look ahead. The angels will support and stand with you as you figure out what is next.

3

angel numbers
0–999

Before we dive into the list of angel numbers, let's look at the difference between single, double, triple, and quadruple numbers, and even longer sequences

Single digits draw our attention to the core components of our lives. The messages here are often broad and want us to tend to foundational aspects of our reality and relationships.

Double digits give us simple directions and affirmations based on where we are in this moment. There are often no juxtapositional forces in play beyond the hoops we make up for ourselves to jump through.

Triple digits point to more than one way through complex situations and relationships. There could be more interference with multiple interests and paths entwining.

Quadruple digits show up in times of intense flow, signifying graduation or completion of a lesson at our current level of consciousness. In the "school" of life, we might encounter this lesson in every season at a higher and higher level of understanding.

Longer sequences are advanced and can hold many messages at once. They should be broken into the smaller sequences you see within them and then be treated akin to words in a sentence. Not every word in a sentence carries the same meaning or impact on the overall meaning. When dealing with longer sequences look for the message that aligns most with your situation, and if the same numbers or groups of numbers are showing up a lot, that part of the message is the most important.

0	New possibilities are coming your way. Pause and reset to be ready for them.
1	It all starts with you. Clarify your mind, actions, and focus.
2	Look for the invitation. What would be fun to do?
3	Trust that the angels are on your side in all endeavors.
4	Every change brings you closer to your highest calling.
5	You are never alone; allow the angels to show up in unexpected ways.
6	Let your heart be part of all your actions and communication.
7	Trust the messages and signs you're seeing.
8	Be authentic in your expression and choices.
9	Let go of what no longer serves you.

10	Let what wants to be made through you meet no resistance.
11	You're always one with your path; be patient as it unfolds.
12	Be discerning of your circle of influence.
13	You have voiced a desire for change, and your request is being met.
14	Invest in your connections and community.
15	You create beauty and are worthy of love by simply existing.
16	Have faith in yourself and the dreams you hold closest to your heart.
17	This is a point of no return; a memorable moment in your life is about to unfold.
18	This is the culmination of a journey or a relationship.
19	The angels of joy are here to imbue your life with magic.
20	Trust the timing of your life.
21	Be ambitious in how many seeds you plant for the future.
22	Holding on to past failures will not help. Let go of the past.
23	Let the angels protect you. Allow them to enfold you in their safety and calmness.
24	All your relationships are a reflection of your union with your own higher self.
25	You are not a novice in this world. Acknowledge the work you have done.
26	Invest in your own counsel.
27	Lead your battles from the front with an open heart.
28	Let all pretense fall when it comes to your ambitions and dreams.

29	Trust that all the right doors are open and all the wrong ones are closed.
30	Be brave when you dream, and share your goals with the Universe.
31	In moments of doubt, know that the best is yet to come.
32	Grab the hands that want to help and carry you.
33	There are so many angels lined up to help you on your journey. Let them support you.
34	Reach higher than ever before, and let old limitations dissolve.
35	A minute of prayer opens more doors than hours of discussion.
36	A higher cause is calling you forward; don't shrink in the presence of your own ambition.
37	The angels are trusting you to create a legacy of love and joy.
38	Avoid neither the valleys nor the peaks of life.
39	The angels want to hear you have faith in yourself as they have faith in you. Speak up!
40	Look at people's actions, not their words.
41	Pay it forward in all areas of your life.
42	Invite the world into your garden, and nurture the flowers that only you can grow.
43	Trust that you have the power to stand alone: you will soon be joined by other visionaries.
44	Spending time alone and in contemplation will open you up to angelic guidance.

45	The finish line is in sight. Reflect on what note you want to end this on.
46	Your life is not measured in length but in depth. Go deeper.
47	The Divine is looking through your eyes; let it enjoy the view.
48	Trust that you've chosen the right teachers for this moment.
49	Honor your own inner child by letting them out to play.
50	Be of service to inspiration and hope.
51	Pick your battles wisely. Not all insults deserve your response.
52	If you have lost your way, start feeding yourself love through every action of self-care that feels good.
53	Enjoy the gift of perspective that is unfolding; these periods in life are precious.
54	You were born with the power to handle this; now, carry the wisdom earned forward.
55	An air of recognition is circling you; let yourself be seen, heard, and celebrated by those around you.
56	Time moves differently for our souls than for our human minds. Trust the timing of your life.
57	You're part of the infinite intelligence and playfulness of the Universe. Enjoy!
58	What would you change today if nothing stood in your way?
59	You are never alone; know that the Universe is unified in its plans for your joy.
60	Elevate your connections to a level of sacredness; only the best belong in your circle of confidants.
61	Your point of view and contribution are needed.

62	Put down what once was a privilege but has now become a burden.
63	You have benevolent powers on your side.
64	The ones who believe they are chosen will see that choice bear fruit.
65	Your sensitivity is a gift.
66	Arrange your life for maximum satisfaction and enjoyment.
67	Do not argue with change; embrace it.
68	Listen to your own voice.
69	Let love rule and everything else dissolve.
70	Allow any emotion to move through you uninterrupted.
71	Trust that your inner wisdom will guide you to the right decisions.
72	Let go of what no longer serves you to make way for new opportunities.
73	Savor this moment, and let the energy ripple through your existence.
74	Believe in your own abilities, and trust that you are capable of achieving great things.
75	You are a spiritual being having a human experience. Trust your intuition and inner guidance.
76	You have the power to create your own reality.
77	The angels are delivering messages and signs through everyone around you.
78	Allow patience and rest when it's needed.
79	Stay grounded and focused on your goals, even in the face of adversity.

80	Embrace change and transformation; it will lead to positive growth and new beginnings.
81	Trust that the Universe is conspiring to bring you what you desire.
82	Cultivate loving relationships with yourself and others.
83	Believe that you are on the right path, and trust that your journey is unfolding perfectly.
84	The angels are confident in your abilities.
85	You are surrounded by abundance and prosperity.
86	Nurture the feeling of appreciation for everything in your life.
87	Stay true to yourself, and do not be swayed by the opinions of others.
88	Avoid letting yourself be guided by fear of judgment by others. You are worthy of all your desires.
89	The Divine is listening: voice your desires out loud.
90	Make space for angelic intervention.
91	Be adventurous and take risks. You're supported by the Universe.
92	No one can take away what is meant for you.
93	Tap into your imagination, and allow yourself to dream big.
94	Embrace the expansion ahead.
95	Believe that everything is working out in your favor, and stay focused on your goals.
96	Focus on maintaining a balance between work and play in your life.
97	No one can bring your ideas to life but you.

98	Trust your instincts and follow your heart, even if it may seem unconventional to others.
99	End the relationships and contracts that have run their course. Something better is on its way.
100	Believe that you have the power to create the life you desire, and take action on your dreams.
101	Become one with the will of your higher self, and let your intuition direct any action.
102	When the lesson is done, move on with grace and gratitude.
103	Enjoy the ride that you're about to embark on, and let the Divine move through you.
104	The angels are proud to witness your progress.
105	Forgive the people who have let you down.
106	No matter the speed of your life, everything happens in Divine timing.
107	See yourself in the best possible light. You're doing the best you can.
108	Release negative thought patterns and beliefs that hold you back from the next steps.
109	Your prayers are being heard.
110	Let yourself be held by the angels.
111	Speak with integrity, and follow through with what you want to create.
112	Your solar plexus is being worked on to open it to more self-acceptance and joy.
113	Celebrate your independence from previous restrictions.
114	Find fulfillment in your own originality.

115	Trust that you are loved and supported by the Universe and all those around you.
116	Your tenacity will be rewarded.
117	Courage and originality are needed for your next endeavors.
118	Your creative expression is needed in this world.
119	What a loss if we didn't get to see your brilliance. Let your light shine.
120	Embrace your ambitions and initiative.
121	Let your heart bloom and fill with gratitude for what you have already accomplished.
122	Your journey is one of power and integrity; don't shy away from your calling.
123	The angels are waiting for you to step forward. Claim your light.
124	Your sensitivity is a precious part of you; protect it.
125	The Universe is always on your side.
126	Take inventory of what would serve your next steps.
127	You have been hiding; step out so love can find you.
128	Your presence is powerful; be clear in your interactions and communication with others.
129	Take care of yourself, and let the angels take care of you.
130	Connect with the trailblazers who came before you.
131	Not all connections are meant to travel with you forever. Allow people to follow their own path.
132	There are shifts happening in your heart connections and relationships. It will be for the best.

133	The most perfect idea to follow is the one that lights up your heart.
134	Trust that you are on the right path, and keep moving forward.
135	You are moving up in the world. Celebrate this moment!
136	Be honest with yourself. What do you truly need?
137	Slow down; nothing is going to pass you by.
138	Listen to the teacher within.
139	You are plugged into the source of all that is; let yourself recharge.
140	You are perfect in the eyes of the Divine.
141	How can you treat your body and physical reality as an altar to the Divine?
142	Be comfortable with the sense of being on a different track than your peers.
143	Choose love over fear and doubts.
144	What you are longing for is already on its way to you.
145	Take back any power you've let others believe they were entitled to wield over you.
146	Allow yourself to feel deeply, and your emotions will reveal the truth of the situation.
147	Your career could take a turn at this time, and you will be presented with new opportunities.
148	Release control of the need to steer every area of your life; the angels are taking over.
149	Trust that you have the power to manifest your dreams and desires.
150	You are being surrounded by love and care from the angels.

151	Look beyond the issues holding you back. Focus on the feeling of achieving the goal.
152	Go within; all the answers are already there.
153	Your previous sacrifices are no longer needed to move up and out of the current situation.
154	Honor the growth you have gone through.
155	No one's advice is as valuable as your own heart.
156	Prioritize your needs and nurture yourself.
157	Your curiosity will be rewarded.
158	Look for balance in your physical reality and surroundings at this time.
159	Use this time to speak to the angels directly; they are listening.
160	Don't get trapped focusing exclusively on the physical world. Prioritize your spirituality.
161	Focus on maintaining a balance between your physical and spiritual needs.
162	Take your interests and goals seriously.
163	The closer you get to the Divine, the clearer the message gets.
164	Create anchors for your goals through smell, touch, taste, and sight. Use physical objects as reminders.
165	Peace within is always available; breathe and slow down to connect with it.
166	Respect your mind-body-spirit connection. Each part of you needs to be honored.
167	Your success helps others see new possibilities. Don't hide your light.

168	You have been distracted by external issues. Come back to your center.
169	Trust that the Universe is supporting you in all aspects of your life.
170	Use everything you've got to get to the next level. Every part of you is invited to join.
171	Be the angel for someone else today, and share your energy with the world.
172	Be present in as many moments as possible. Don't miss out on your life.
173	Spend time with nature, children, or animals to connect with your heart.
174	You are the creator of this moment. Think bigger!
175	Focus on the positive aspects of your life and possibilities.
176	Take a break, but don't lose momentum for long.
177	Many messages are coming through. Journal about what you are receiving.
178	Focus on what you can control, and let the rest go.
179	Seek new perspectives on your current situation.
180	The past can teach you much about how your next steps will play out.
181	Trust that you are being guided toward your soul's purpose.
182	Show others how to treat you by showing yourself love each day.
183	The earth you inhabit is one of your teachers; honor it.
184	You have hidden talents yet to be explored. Try something new today.

185	Don't close your mind to new experiences and opportunities.
186	Clear your energy of anything that should no longer be connected to you.
187	There is more to the current situation than your mind knows; meditate to learn more.
188	Be careful to not put others down when you share your opinions and visions.
189	Don't hold back or fear being too much for others. You are perfect the way you are.
190	Shift your energy by making new and different choices at this time.
191	Desire is part of the human experience. Allow it to show you what feels good to you.
192	Fear is not a good guide; have faith that the angels would not have led you astray.
193	Trust that everything is happening for your highest good.
194	Treat the gifts and information you receive with reverence.
195	You will never stop growing; take responsibility for each step you take forward.
196	Let new connections and ideas meet your open mind.
197	Don't get stuck in an either-or kind of thinking; there is more than one solution here.
198	Get to it. Nothing but doubts are holding you back.
199	Find the joy from your inner child, and allow it to influence your goals.
200	Focus on cultivating more peace in your everyday life.

201	Be discerning with the people you honor with your friendship.
202	Don't let others take advantage of your kindness.
203	Be more gentle toward the flaws you see in others; they are an invitation to self-reflect.
204	Become the peacemaker you wished for earlier in your life.
205	Cooperate with the ideas that come to you at this time.
206	Pick diplomacy over confrontation when possible.
207	This is a moment to surrender yourself to what is trying to be felt through you.
208	You cannot fail as long as you follow your own authentic path.
209	How can you up the devotion you show to the people around you?
210	Believe that you're deserving of success and abundance; the Universe is supporting you.
211	Understand that the duality you are experiencing is necessary for the cultivation of empathy.
212	Attention to detail will benefit you at this time.
213	There is a loving presence around you; if you feel called to pray, the angels are listening.
214	Don't isolate yourself from the ebb and flow of life and your relationships.
215	Rest assured that all will turn out for the highest good.
216	You are worthy of a fulfilling and happy life.
217	Be at peace with yourself and your surroundings.

218	Putting boundaries around your availability and attention is an act of self-love.
219	Focus on the people and places that make you happy.
220	Be ambitious in your artistic and intuitive pursuits.
221	You are worthy of respect and kindness.
222	Speak of yourself with respect and care. Be generous with yourself before giving to others.
223	Don't allow your relationships to become one-way streets from either side.
224	Grace is a state that expands to fill the space you give it in your life.
225	Do it even if the payoff will be less than you thought. Do it for the experience.
226	Be playful and flirt with a deeper level of spiritual devotion to your own ideas.
227	Quiet your mind. You have let others fill you with their words and energy. Release the ideas that aren't yours.
228	You are a creator of the energy around you. Look at how you talk to yourself.
229	Self-doubt is normal. Don't let it hold you back from your goals.
230	Trust that your hard work and dedication will bring you success.
231	There is a new level of spirituality and connection with your higher self available to you.
232	You live among the realized ideas and inspiration of your previous goals. Be grateful!

233	You are creating more obstacles than necessary; look for an easier way.
234	This moment is not about being the best; let yourself redefine success in this situation.
235	Document your thoughts, experiences, and physical reality at this time. Your future self will want to look back.
236	Spend time with someone you love today. Share your heart with them.
237	Use your intuition more than the advice of others. The angels speak through you.
238	You are surrounded by people who love and support you.
239	Forgive yourself for past mistakes.
240	Be kind to others; they are going through their own challenges.
241	New information is coming through. Make time for inspiration to strike.
242	Release the trauma, suffering, and pain that you have been carrying for others.
243	Seek out nature and the sound of water to help clear away negative thoughts.
244	Express gratitude for all the opportunities that come your way.
245	Look for the good in others.
246	Prepare for the good that you wish for by making space in your life for it.
247	Keep going and ignore the people who want to redirect you.
248	If you are not lit up by your current situation, put a deadline on how long you'll stay in it.

249	The unknown is part of the plan. Many of the next steps will feel new and possibly strange.
250	Speak up for others. Be part of the conversation, and offer the solutions you see.
251	Share your abundance and energy with the world.
252	Question if you are operating on outdated information. Try out new approaches.
253	Allow yourself to turn down and disappoint people. Boundaries are love in action.
254	Want more energy? Spend more energy on things you love.
255	You can't go back. There is no path that leads to the past.
256	Step up your self-care, not the demands you put on yourself.
257	There are messages trying to get through. Make space for contemplation.
258	Believe in the power of positivity, and focus on what you want to create in your life.
259	Be open to receiving all the blessings the Universe offers.
260	You are constantly improving and growing. Celebrate each step on the journey!
261	Don't betray yourself in service to causes that don't align fully with your soul.
262	Observe the world from a different vantage point today.
263	Plan your approach, and make sure you have all your ducks in a row.
264	Your third eye is opening. Allow the wisdom to flow through it into your life.

265	Don't let yourself get interrupted by distractions; remove what does not serve you.
266	Your family and chosen community are important at this time; spend time with them.
267	You can't fully grasp the magnitude of your impact on the world. What you create is needed.
268	Create reminders to get back on track, making recentering a daily occurrence.
269	Be the first one to reach out if you feel that spark of connection.
270	You are capable of creating a life you love. Take action!
271	If something is off course, make the necessary adjustments.
272	You have more than one way of connecting with the Divine. Develop new ways of listening.
273	Be honest with others about what drives you.
274	Take a moment to think things through in order to respond with integrity and care.
275	You are not in a rush. Take your time.
276	Let your flexibility be an asset; things are shifting.
277	Step forward and teach what you know; embody the teachings you share.
278	Be clear in your intention and communication.
279	You are a magnet for success and abundance.
280	Release negative self-talk by reflecting on what it keeps you safe from pursuing.
281	You have new priorities in your life. Create space for them to flourish.

282	Visualize what the next cycle of your life will look and feel like.
283	Initiate exchange and interaction with others.
284	Receive compliments and praise with grace.
285	You need new goals. Journal on what they could be.
286	You know yourself better than you think. Make aligned choices.
287	Build on the strong foundation you've already created.
288	You are capable of overcoming any obstacle in your way.
289	Redirection is coming down from on high. Allow the angels to guide you.
290	Pain is a teacher we all share. Embrace the lesson to move on.
291	When you recognize good advice, make sure to appreciate the messenger.
292	Co-create with the Universe today, and speak your joy into existence.
293	Help heal others by sharing your wisdom.
294	Patience is a necessity at this time.
295	Honesty is always rewarded in the end.
296	Pay attention to what people rely on you for.
297	Waiting on others to open the doors is keeping you small.
298	Detach from the drama around you.
299	Look for a peaceful solution.
300	Get excited; new energy and joy are coming your way.
301	Seek out information and resources on the energy you want to embody and experience.

302	Be simple in your requests.
303	Create a sacred space to connect with your ancestors today.
304	You are deserving of love and happiness.
305	If you are holding back from sharing your point of view, you are depriving the world of your brilliance.
306	Embody the energy that you want to experience more often.
307	Be proud of your accomplishments.
308	Spend your energy where it is appreciated.
309	Trust that your positive attitude will attract abundance and blessings.
310	Face the fears that hold you back.
311	Your purpose shifts over time; let it be what it wants to be.
312	You are capable of achieving anything you set your mind to.
313	Replenish your energy before giving it to others.
314	Future you is proud of what you're planning to do. It will work out.
315	You are further than you think.
316	You are worthy of love and happiness.
317	Be assertive and clear in your communication.
318	Apologize to those you have hurt.
319	You are not beholden to any previous version of yourself.
320	If a truth has emerged that changes the situation, embrace it.
321	Relationships are not supposed to stay the same. Let them evolve.
322	The angels love to see you expand.

323	This is a teaching moment for your soul.
324	Mastery comes through the willingness to fail repeatedly.
325	You are keeping yourself stuck. Move out of the way.
326	Get rid of old decisions and clutter.
327	There are many ways of showing love. You can love without being close to that person.
328	Transitions are always Divinely guided.
329	Thank the people who have helped you on this journey.
330	You are never without support.
331	You are surrounded by people who uplift and inspire you.
332	Your spiritual gifts are meant to be shared.
333	Use your words to build a better world for all. Trust that you have luck on your side.
334	Release what does not belong in your new reality.
335	Your curiosity is trying to show you something new
336	Let yourself be loved.
337	Ground yourself to the earth today.
338	Sleep and rest are part of the cycle of creation.
339	Each new version of you needs to be celebrated.
340	Reward yourself for the work you've done.
341	You will overcome everything standing in your way.
342	What you once found hard is getting easier by the day.
343	Your connection to your higher self can never be cut off, only forgotten for a time.
344	Take a step back and check in with yourself before moving ahead.

345	Don't accumulate what does not serve you or bring you joy.
346	Thrust yourself into the fire of your own heart. Embrace the passion within.
347	You are surrounded by beauty and positivity.
348	Take inventory of your positive traits and how they can serve you more.
349	Let go of what wants to leave.
350	Each of your prayers is being answered in the best way for your soul's evolution.
351	Seek out what excited you as a child.
352	Celebrate the success of others.
353	Be sincere in your interactions.
354	You are connected to the highest levels of the Divine. Never doubt your place in the Universe.
355	Honor your need for safety at this time.
356	New angels are joining your team at this time.
357	Trust that you have the strength and courage to overcome any obstacle.
358	You are impacting the world in positive ways every day.
359	Be honest about the amount of energy you're willing to give.
360	You can rely on yourself whenever needed.
361	Your internal compass is always right.
362	You are becoming more powerful each day.
363	The things that fall away were never meant to stay.
364	You are encouraged to embrace and embody ease.

365	Pay attention to what you're already doing to support the future version of you.
366	Your words have so much power. Speak with intention.
367	Listen to the words you share with the Universe through all your conversations.
368	Starting over is a gift not everyone gets.
369	Your power will grow with the level of responsibility you take for it.
370	You are worthy of all the good things in your life.
371	When you have more, give more. Continue the cycle of abundance.
372	Love is never lost; your heart has space for everything it has ever held.
373	Stability is needed at this time; tend to your foundations.
374	A new chapter means a new outlook on life.
375	Own your confidence; you've earned it.
376	Fail and fail again on the journey to mastery.
377	Your values are important for the level of satisfaction you can achieve. Honor them.
378	Move things around in your physical space today. Shifts are needed.
379	Believe that you are worthy of love and abundance. Good things are coming your way.
380	Clarify the goals that you want your new habits to help you toward.
381	Follow the flow of your creativity.
382	Certain things are out of your hands. Proceed with caution.

383	Give out what you want to receive.
384	Invite yourself on a date with your future self, and visualize what that looks like.
385	Stay clear of situations that you know are beyond your current capabilities.
386	Call attention to the needs of others, and amplify the messages you believe in.
387	Be confident in your ability to overcome challenges.
388	Your subconscious beliefs need some attention; look for the origin story of your limits.
389	You are surrounded by positivity and love.
390	Doing one thing at a time is the best approach right now.
391	The angels are sending people to support you. Look for helpers.
392	Seeking closure doesn't mean you have to relive an experience. Let the door close.
393	Intensity is part of transmutation. Allow things to change.
394	Create space for more abundance in all areas of your life.
395	Embrace all facets of your expression.
396	What felt right once might not be the right fit any longer. Embrace the shift.
397	In conflict, speak with the other person's higher self to see the core of the issue.
398	You are creating the path as you walk it. Each step is a victory in its own right.
399	Pick a sign, symbol, or word that represents your goals. The angels will show you the way.

400	Talk yourself up! There is a need to clean up your internal language.
401	Your triggers are indicators of unclaimed desires. Examine and embrace them.
402	Release yourself from the physical things that keep you from moving on.
403	Track your creative and intuitive energy and what it looks like at different stages of the day.
404	Your family will not always be your biggest supporter. Cultivate your circle of friends.
405	You are a strong and resilient person. Reframe any challenges into opportunities.
406	Follow the nudges you get to be introduced to a new spiritual tool or experience.
407	Someone around you needs support. Reach out to the person that popped into your mind.
408	Affirmations are a boundary against old patterns and thoughts. Utilize them.
409	Absolve yourself of old guilt by releasing others from your own resentment.
410	Look for the good in others.
411	Do not put limits on the level of pleasure you're allowed to experience in your life.
412	Allow good things into your life on a daily basis.
413	You are surrounded by love and support. Everything will work out for your highest good.
414	Meet people halfway. There is magic in collaboration.
415	Notice the beauty in the world around you. It is everywhere.

416	Your name is being spoken aloud in places of influence.
417	Donate your time to places or people who could benefit from your care.
418	Perfection is a distraction from creation.
419	Give with no expectation of return beyond the joy of helping others.
420	Love has found a home in your heart. Nurture it.
421	Your crown chakra is opening. Let it anchor into your highest self's vision for your life.
422	Sit with the overwhelm or confusion you feel. It will pass when you let it speak.
423	Look at what you have already achieved and experienced, and be grateful.
424	There are no limits here. Expand.
425	Invite the angels into your life, and let them help you with the smallest tasks.
426	There is more than one right option here. Sleep on it.
427	Listen to new people, music, ideas, and thoughts today.
428	It is all right to leave old ideas behind.
429	A new teacher is emerging in your field.
430	Trust that you are making the right choices.
431	You are contributing to the elevation of the universal vibration.
432	Spend time with people younger in mind than you today.
433	You are capable of achieving your dreams.
434	Any questions asked with an open heart will be answered in time.

435	New pathways of abundance are opening up.
436	Light a candle or fire for the people whose shoulders you stand upon today.
437	Treat yourself better. You are deserving of all that you desire.
438	Your creativity is looking for a new outlet.
439	Clarity is a gift that comes from action.
440	You have reached a new level of understanding. Look at everything again.
441	Small actions matter. Don't discount your efforts.
442	Clean and change things in around your desk, workspace, or kitchen to get new energy.
443	The ripples of your current actions are creating new opportunities ahead.
444	Take responsibility for your learning and progress; being the first at something gives you a spotlight to illuminate the path for others.
445	You are holding on to grudges. Hand over the situation to the Divine.
446	Reach out to the person you're thinking of.
447	Envision the biggest return on your efforts possible, and so it is.
448	Be honest with yourself and others about your feelings.
449	You are responsible for your own energy.
450	When you thrive, you make that energy available to others without any extra effort.
451	Reevaluate your approach to love and romantic relationships.

452	Your confidence is an aspect of your self-worth that is meant to expand over time.
453	You deserve everything glorious and good that's showing up.
454	You are letting abundance wait on your doorstep; clear the way for it.
455	Your container for happiness is expanding.
456	Clean your physical space to invigorate your energy.
457	You are so very needed in the world.
458	Spread gratitude and appreciation in all the spaces you move through.
459	You are surrounded by abundance and prosperity in all areas of your life.
460	Your physical body holds the key to your next level of fulfillment and joy.
461	Be confident in your ability to make the right decisions.
462	What is breaking down will lead to a breakthrough.
463	Your time and energy are never wasted; focus on the lessons learned.
464	Be vulnerable with the people you want to build solid relationships with.
465	A deeper love is available to you. Create space for intimacy and romance.
466	Cut the cords on the old hurt—no need to carry it further.
467	Up your visibility in the areas in which you're looking to grow.
468	Your natural inclinations and interests are guideposts toward a meaningful life.

469	Accept that people will meet you where they are.
470	You're unique and worthy of celebration and love as you are in this very moment.
471	You have been in this situation before, but you are not the same person as then.
472	Extend the same unconditional love to yourself as you give to others.
473	Look deeper at the ideas you have around worthiness and work.
474	Take better care of the abundance you have already received.
475	A previous rejection can be seen in a new light now.
476	You are surrounded by peace and tranquility.
477	The fear you feel is an indicator of past loss, not the current issue.
478	Your intuition is more valuable than others' experience.
479	You are preparing for greater things. Do the work in front of you.
480	Be grateful for your inner strength and resilience.
481	It is time to embrace the next level of your career and ambition.
482	The angels are working through every available channel for your highest good.
483	Your joy is contagious. Don't hide it.
484	Your past mistakes are impacting your self-image. Forgive your younger self.
485	Things are shifting. Let your priorities evolve and change with them.

486	You have repressed an important part of your identity to fit in. Own your full expression.
487	Your future is looking lighter by the minute.
488	You have neglected your need to daydream. Spend time with your imagination today.
489	Seek out new experiences, art, and interactions to find new inspiration.
490	Your inner rebel needs to be included in your plans.
491	Take a nap or break from the situation, and come back when your mind is clear.
492	You are constantly attracting positivity and success.
493	Ask others for feedback on your strongest qualities and gifts. Let yourself be seen.
494	Your current challenges will not have an enduring impact on your life. Take it easy.
495	Treat yourself and others with kindness and understanding.
496	You are holding on too strongly to an issue. Let it go and it will resolve.
497	Create new routines and boundaries around encounters that drain you.
498	Your heart is trying to tell you something. Slow down and listen.
499	Observe your inner monologue for deeper insight into your current situation.
500	The angels are connecting you to unseen helpers on more levels than ever.
501	Believe in yourself and your intuition. Trust that you will make the right decisions.

502	Fear is an advisor that will always keep you small.
503	You are choosing to ignore messages that could shift your whole reality.
504	Listen to the advice you give to others as that wisdom applies to you too.
505	Journal about your next steps and what is holding you back.
506	Your body is doing everything it can to keep you safe. Treat it kindly.
507	You might be creating more work for yourself at this time.
508	Let joy be your guide.
509	Document the limits you see in yourself when communicating with others.
510	More love wants to reach you. Make plans to gather people together.
511	Your higher self is a better advisor than any medium. Create space for meditation.
512	Trust the journey of your life, and have faith in the Universe's plan for you.
513	Your fear of the next step is delaying your spiritual development.
514	Spread the word about the people and places you love to others.
515	Your heart chakra is being worked on. Let any stuck emotion out.
516	Your mind is stuck on an unhelpful train of thought. Seek out new input.
517	You can handle the change that is happening around you.

518	See your commitments through to the end. Be true to your word.
519	Use your gifts efficiently, and prioritize the way you can make the most impact.
520	Check in with your mental and emotional well-being. Adjust accordingly.
521	Accept the message that wants to come through; it is important.
522	Your fears are obscuring your worldview. Examine their validity.
523	Seek out new inspiration for your next steps.
524	The proof you are looking for is just external validation. Trust your inner guidance.
525	Revisit an old favorite work of art or literature to get reinspired.
526	You are free to follow any path that feels right for you.
527	Bestow blessings on others.
528	Your fear of being controlled is stopping you from moving forward.
529	Delays are redirections.
530	Express yourself freely and authentically.
531	You can now connect more deeply with the spiritual masters of your lineage.
532	Your prayers have been heard. Have faith that everything is unfolding perfectly.
533	Treat yourself with the kindness others have denied you.

534	By underestimating yourself you keep others from seeing your light.
535	Commit fully to building the community and family of your dreams.
536	You have excellent helpers on your team. Let them work for you.
537	Ground yourself deeply into the love of the Universe.
538	Remember the journey that led you here. Each step was necessary for what comes next.
539	Honor the sensitivity and creativity within you.
540	Illusions are falling, and the truth of the situation will soon be clear.
541	Honor your need for rest and downtime. Release yourself from the expectations of others.
542	Ask for the miracles that would help the most at this time.
543	You are back at a familiar place, but you can choose to gain a new perspective on it.
544	Change is a constant companion of life. Embrace it.
545	Believe that you are a powerful co-creator with the Universe.
546	You have the ability to manifest your desires.
547	The closer you get to your true path, the more support you will feel.
548	You are hanging on to physical things and blocking the space needed for new blessings.
549	Reveal a side of yourself that you deem flawed. There is healing in sharing.

550	Trust the information you receive in between the words of your conversations.
551	You are becoming aware of what is the most important area to focus on right now.
552	Psychic gifts are showing up and will benefit from support and further development.
553	You are held back by the habit of studying when you should be teaching others.
554	Isolation is a survival tactic that has run its course. Reach out to others.
555	Your communication and exchange with the world are continuously improving as your impact reaches even further.
556	Your inner light is getting brighter, and more people and opportunities are coming your way.
557	The work you are doing is healing those behind and ahead in your lineage too.
558	Explore the language you use around your desires, and speak them into existence.
559	Model a positive leadership style by being encouraging and direct with your vision.
560	When silenced, reflect on what you're being protected from by not speaking.
561	Give yourself credit for the changes you are making.
562	There is a deep layer of protection and love around you at this time.
563	The most fleeting connection can have a profound impact.
564	You are trying to force the timing of your dreams. Let go and the angels will sort it out.

565	Your current obstacle was created for maximum learning potential. Look at the big picture.
566	You deserve all the miracles and blessings waiting in the wings. Allow them in.
567	Your guardian angel is reaching out. Spend time in meditation to connect deeper.
568	There is a need for consistency and follow-through at this time.
569	Step away from the interactions and connections that deplete you.
570	Your energy is being released from old contacts and agreements.
571	Dreams are a space to connect with your teachers in spirit. Set an intention to meet them.
572	Celebrate the moves of the Universe as they always get you closer to the next level.
573	You are always protected and cared for.
574	Trust is a state that is cultivated through leaps of faith.
575	Ask for your karma to be released in the most perfect way for you at this time.
576	What is broken was never meant to stay in your energy field forever.
577	You are keeping a part of your heart closed off from yourself. Let it be opened now.
578	There is no test when it comes to love, only lessons learned in an ever-deepening way.
579	Self-acceptance is part of growing into the next version of yourself.

580	The angels are calling for more healing within your relationship with your parents.
581	Align yourself with a state of joy and contentment.
582	Create space for deeper work with the angels by dedicating more time to yourself.
583	Work with the energy levels and cycles of your body.
584	All your connections are blessed by the angels.
585	Your soul is trying to get your attention. Spend time in nature and meditation to connect.
586	You are living the very best version of your life; yet more blessings are still on their way.
587	Maintain a journal on your ideas and inspiration. The muses enjoy an already working artist.
588	You have a positive impact on the world and the space around you.
589	The next step is an internal one.
590	You were born to light the way for others.
591	The road ahead mirrors the road within you. Put energy into both.
592	Devote part of your day to the pleasure of your senses. Be fully present.
593	You have forgotten your own power; call it back.
594	Take inventory of the people who have helped you get to where you are now. Say thank you.
595	Be grateful for your health and well-being.
596	Contemplate the pros and cons of each choice in front of you before moving ahead.

597	The path in front of you is being cleared and illuminated by the angels.
598	Stay true to your original goal even when the path gets challenging.
599	The information you are looking for will come through an unlikely person or interaction.
600	Treat your body and home as an extension of your energy field. Clear away the old.
601	Joy is cultivated through self-acceptance and the pursuit of wonder.
602	Your abilities are not gifts that can be taken away. They are fully part of your being.
603	You are making things more complicated than they need to be. Simplify your life.
604	You are constantly attracting positivity into your life.
605	Enjoy where you are at this moment in your life. There is no need to look too far ahead.
606	You're drawing in love, opportunities, and support with every step you take forward.
607	Focus on your spiritual growth. The angels encourage you to stay open.
608	Be cautious about the opportunities that look great but are not aligned with your goals.
609	You are being presented with multiple options. Choose with your heart.
610	You can never lose the love that was meant to be part of your life.

611	Be aware of old cynicism coloring your present experiences. This is a new day.
612	Show up for the tough conversations, and be honest with yourself and others.
613	You are having an influx of angelic support and guidance for the foreseeable future.
614	Your maternal lineage is witnessing you becoming more and more powerful.
615	Make space for ease, fun, and joy in your days.
616	Not everything is in your control. Let the Universe figure out the next few steps.
617	You deserve to be cherished for the unique light you are in the world.
618	Identify the limits you put on yourself when it comes to receiving love.
619	Your spirit team is adding their prayers and energy to yours right now.
620	The more you release old fears, emotions, and beliefs, the easier the next doors will open.
621	You are being slowed down to take a second pass at an issue from your past.
622	The right choice is the one that draws you in and lights you up.
623	You will be receiving more messages and signs from your ancestors at this time.
624	Your emotions and sensitivity are working in your favor.
625	Your sense of responsibility can lead you to take on more than necessary.

A LITTLE BIT OF ANGEL NUMBERS

626	Your throat chakra is being worked on. Let your voice be heard.
627	You're being shown new levels of connection between your physical body and spiritual self.
628	Return the energy that does not belong to you. Cut cords to feel free.
629	You are the biggest contributor to your own well-being.
630	Be mindful of the emotions and mental state of others. Your words have an impact.
631	The angels would never allow you to get too far off track. Trust the guidance you hear.
632	There is a higher reason for the encounters and connections you make. Show up as you.
633	You are healing old patterns within your family and spiritual lineage.
634	Be proud of the healing you have done around your heart.
635	Every person you let into your life becomes part of the feedback loop on your growth.
636	Cut the cords on the people and spaces that no longer serve you.
637	Inner serenity is created by weathering many a storm; you will get through this.
638	You are cheered on by countless angels.
639	Other people's perspective is more objective than yours at this time. Hear them out.
640	You never stop growing closer to the Divine.
641	Call on protection and support whenever you need a little extra boost of angelic love.

642	Obstacles are being removed. Stand aside and let the angels work for you.
643	This is a time to throw everything at a dream or challenge, and you're holding back.
644	You are being guided to pursue a higher level of learning at this time.
645	There are angels assigned to your corner of the earth. Let them help you feel at home.
646	Your inner artist wants to be inspired. Take yourself on an adventure.
647	You have the power to transform the lives of those around you. Own your influence.
648	Hand it all over to the angels. With their help anything is possible.
649	Rise above any pettiness and disappointment; it will not lead you where you want to go.
650	Not everyone from this chapter of your life is worthy of going with you to the next one.
651	Your wildness is an integral part of who you are. Don't put it in a cage.
652	If you want to be honored, honor the Divine in others.
653	Measuring your success and progress against others can be a distraction from enjoying your blessings.
654	Accept the help offered, and let yourself rest.
655	You have felt disconnected from spirit; it is time to get back in touch with your angels.
656	The spotlight is coming your way. Let it find you ready to shine.

657	Make those you love part of your plans for expansion.
658	Take inventory of the beliefs that hold you back, and bless each one as you let them go.
659	Holding back serves no one. You only fail if you do not try.
660	Your personal spiritual team is proud of you.
661	Become one with love. Become one with your own heart. Become one with the Divine.
662	The angels are placing their warm hands on the back of your heart. Let their love in.
663	Be the bringer of light and positivity in all the spaces you move through.
664	Synchronicities are the angels' way of being seen. Follow your bliss.
665	You don't need to know every detail of the next step. Leave some space for Divine surprises.
666	Your relationships are here to make you more aware and available to what wants to be felt and birthed through you.
667	Getting off track does not mean leaving the field for good. Get back in the game.
668	Your vision for the future is changing. Allow yourself to focus on the best outcome for all.
669	Your level of manifestation will be raised as you let go of emotionally draining people.
670	Focus on what will support you, and embrace the person you're becoming as a result.
671	Your confidence has been shaken, but your recovery is aided by the Divine.

672	Recognize the value you bring to the relationships you are building.
673	Your prayers have been heard, and new support and guidance is coming your way.
674	Both physical and spiritual travel plans are shifting, and this new journey is the right one.
675	Draw on the strength of those who came before you. They lend their power willingly.
676	Bless the spaces you move through.
677	Embrace the present moment and the miracle it is to be alive.
678	You can embody peace when you or someone else is in need of it.
679	New abilities and gifts are coming through. They will show up in your dreams first.
680	Get to know yourself deeper to embrace the Divine work you're here to do.
681	Your willpower is needed in your creative pursuits.
682	The splinter of fear you have yet to deal with is interfering with your ability to receive.
683	Speak up. The message coming through is for others as much as it is for your own ears.
684	Thank you for becoming more and more you! The angels are happy with your progress.
685	Be thorough when dealing with this obstacle. As you clear it a new path appears.
686	Old lessons are being seen in a new light. Be aware of the nuances you can see now.

A LITTLE BIT OF ANGEL NUMBERS

687	Forgive all missteps you have made in the past. You have learned from each one.
688	The journey is yours. Let go of waiting for others to get on board. Lead your own way.
689	What has stagnated in your reality needs your loving attention to bloom again.
690	There is excavation to be done to find the spark of joy that you've been missing.
691	The Divine is always part of the bigger picture. Ask for more clarity to get help seeing it.
692	Your attention has been wandering. Focus on what you want to see made real.
693	Focus on growing what is already in your hands. The rest can wait.
694	You are moving out of a time of darkness. Let the light in.
695	Your kindness ripples through the cosmos in ever-increasing waves. Keep giving.
696	You're being used as an instrument of love and joy. Let the angels direct your actions.
697	Look at the actions of those who say they're helping you. Are they aligned with their words?
698	Envision the best possible outcome for all involved, and work toward that.
699	Support those who rarely ask for it at this time. Be someone's angel today.
700	Your gifts are not an accident; treat them as the blessings they were meant to be.

701	Being misunderstood is a chance to show up even more authentically.
702	Others' authority is no replacement for the voice of your soul. Come back to you.
703	Your sacral chakra is being worked on, allowing more joy and pleasure into your life.
704	By forgiving others you free yourself from patterns of resentment.
705	You are never unworthy in the eyes of the Divine.
706	There is never only one way, and you're never cut off from the guidance you seek.
707	Care for the place you call home at this time, and create a sanctuary of love.
708	The room you make for miracles needs to fit the size of the miracle you're praying for.
709	You're moving on from a fear-based relationship with the Universe. All is love.
710	All the blessings you have shared with others are now coming back to you magnified.
711	Speak out loud about the gifts you see in those around you. Share the praise you seek.
712	Any setback is just a reset. New opportunities and levels are opening up.
713	What can seem like a sacrifice is an opportunity in disguise.
714	Be grateful for the opportunities that come your way.
715	Your feelings are valid and point to a message from your higher self that needs to be heard.

716	Higher levels of angels are taking part in your next level of expansion and growth.
717	Let what wants to leave go. You are always in the company of angels.
718	The next level of your life will mean fully letting go of this one first.
719	You are worthy of a fulfilling and rewarding career.
720	You are going through a deeper awakening of your purpose.
721	Let the Divine be your teacher in trust.
722	Your commitment to joy and pleasure is supported by the angels.
723	Turn away from those who fill your heart with envy and emptiness.
724	You're going through a period of expansion. Uncertainty is part of it.
725	Your life is a never-ending prayer from your highest self to the Divine.
726	Be proud of the healing you have done around your relationships.
727	You are encouraged to revisit experiences from your childhood that are keeping you small.
728	Open the door that feels like the biggest leap of faith. You are ready for it.
729	You are becoming aware of the most important relationships in your life at this time.
730	All conflicts are being solved at the highest level. Work on you, and let people be who they are.
731	Your heart is the center of your power. Let it rule your life.

732	The angels are proud of your willingness to work through the current challenges.
733	Your happiness is connected to the joyous center of all creation.
734	You can never call on the angels too much. Let them hear all of your prayers.
735	Your ancestors are joyful witnesses of your progress.
736	There are aspects of your work and career still left undiscovered. Stay curious.
737	You're working through memories from another life, and releasing them will help your current one.
738	The feminine aspects of your being are being cleared of old assumptions and rejection.
739	The angels are helping you to reconnect and open up to feel a deeper level of joy and fun.
740	Clarify the purpose behind your actions, and eliminate what does not align with your goals.
741	You're never without resources when you rely on the endless abundance of the Universe.
742	You have everything you need to move beyond the current challenges. Go within.
743	Surrender to the path as it is being shown. There are no wrong steps in front of you.
744	What you're asking for is already available to you in spirit. Manifest it through faith.
745	Look at what you're giving out and letting into your life currently. Is it a balanced exchange?

746	There are truths being voiced you haven't heard before. Listen with a receptive heart.
747	New modalities of healing and connection will be brought to your attention by the angels.
748	Prioritize your spiritual practices to nourish your connection to the Divine.
749	What you are healing right now is part of your spiritual growth.
750	Forgive the people who did not honor the eternal light of your inner child.
751	Protect your energy when outside parties are drawing you into pointless drama.
752	Expand the scope of your influence, and go where you are celebrated.
753	Pause and reflect before reacting to what is in front of you. Choose love.
754	Identify the limits you put on yourself when it comes to showing love. Release them.
755	Redirection can be messy. Hand over the reins to the Divine, and take one step at a time.
756	Your body is a connection to the Divine. Honor its needs and capabilities.
757	You are listening to voices of the past. Pray and meditate on higher guidance.
758	Your presence is requested in spaces you've yet to enter. Allow the angels to open new doors.
759	Prepare for the best possible outcome.
760	Big fear means that big breakthroughs and change are possible. Ground yourself.

761	You're letting go of old stories at the perfect pace. Let this healing take the time it needs.
762	Your ancestors are proud of the choices you have made.
763	Call on the teacher within. The answers are inside of you.
764	Share your plans with the Universe, and ask for support at each step.
765	Unburden yourself by sharing your worries with your spiritual team. That is what they are here for.
766	It is never too late to follow the dreams of your heart. Miracles are available to you at any age.
767	Focus on grounding yourself in your body and the present moment.
768	You have yet to take one of the important solo explorations of your soul curriculum. Follow your curiosity.
769	Cherish the connection you have with each part of your spiritual self and what it looks like in your everyday life.
770	Your experiences and reflection are valuable. Share them with others.
771	Regret is a distraction from the lesson at hand. Negative outcomes are invitations from the Divine to strengthen your resolve.
772	You're surrounded by the angels of forgiveness, resolution, and healing. Lean on the support that is being offered.
773	Seek out the counsel of those who have traveled through the same stretch of darkness that you have recently gone through. You're not alone.
774	Satisfaction comes from being deeply intentional with your choices. Do not settle for less than what fills you up.

775	The teacher within you is pushing you toward a larger audience.
776	Portals of possibilities are opening. Spend time in meditation to find the right one to step through.
777	Accept your role and journey as a spiritual light for others.
778	Listen to the nudges you get right before sleeping and when coming awake. Write them down.
779	Security and safety are found within you. Anchoring those feelings will give you a deeper sense of home.
780	Your current relationships will benefit from objective evaluation of your chosen helpers for this level of your life.
781	Create space around and within you for even more abundance and prosperity.
782	The Universe is happy that you're embracing the gifts you were born with.
783	Seeing people as the villain of your story diminishes your own power.
784	Your healing gifts are meant to be used and rewarded in equal measure for their impact on the world.
785	Serving the light of creation means never letting your own light dim for long.
786	Follow-through is part of the success you crave. Keep showing up.
787	Let others pass through the doors of your life without attaching yourself to their energy.
788	You have been unclear in your intentions, and your reality reflects this. Meditate on the certainty and vision needed.

789	You are waiting on people or signs to confirm a choice you have already made. Move forward on your own accord.
790	The angels of ascension are working on your energy. Let yourself be lifted.
791	The Divine Mother within is embracing every part of your being, body and soul.
792	Your paternal lineage is witnessing you becoming more and more powerful.
793	Things going wrong is not a sign that you're off course. Trust the unfolding of your life.
794	Your energy is sacred. Treat it as the precious resource it is.
795	See the light in others, and encourage their flame to burn as brightly as possible.
796	There is always enough for everyone. Others' success is a sign of the inevitability of your own.
797	Healing means lifting and examining everything within your own darkness with soft and caring hands.
798	Your intuition is a lens that gets sharper with consistent use.
799	Spend time discovering and keeping track of how your own energy works and flows.
800	Speak about and draw attention to the bravery of others to ignite it in yourself.
801	You have traveled with part of your current spirit team for many life cycles. Ask to be connected to their accumulated knowledge.
802	No one is truly lost to death or separation. The love that connects you is eternal even if the link is cut in this life.

803	A shift in perception is needed. You can ask for more than you think.
804	Take a moment to reevaluate the plan and its participants. This situation includes some unforeseen bumps in the road.
805	Bless all the abundance you send out to see it returned multiplied.
806	Include the people you love in your visualizations and goals. See them share your joy.
807	There is no way forward without risk, but staying put is its own form of failure.
808	Every new path is an opportunity to let the Divine lead.
809	Stubbornness is control in disguise. Let everything shift for your highest good.
810	Set boundaries. You can be the one others lean on without losing yourself.
811	Thank you for being part of the group that is here to help heal the world and the people in it.
812	This detour is a circle that leads you back to you.
813	Rewards can come in the form of new people and the ideas they share with you.
814	The angels are grateful to be part of your evolution.
815	You belong in a circle of powerful people. Never doubt your place in the world.
816	Hand over your concerns and fears. Nothing is impossible to the Divine.
817	Take a break and rest. It is safe to slow down.
818	Some of your soul contracts are coming to an end at this time.

819	There is always more abundance waiting just around the corner.
820	You know the right thing to do is to embrace the change ahead.
821	Staying in your current situation will be easier if you're fully honest about your emotions and intentions.
822	You are perfect as you are in this moment and every single one following it.
823	Your focus on the practical aspects of your life is blocking the angels from delivering a range of miracles and support.
824	Healing can come in the form of just treating yourself better.
825	Let go of other people's take on God. Your personal connection and understanding of the Divine are being refined.
826	Look for spaces that are uplifting, and spend time in the presence of earthly angels. You belong to that circle too.
827	No path is easy all the time, but even struggles can be joyful when shared with your angels.
828	Let the lessons and wisdom you have gathered so far spill into all areas of your life. How you expand one way is how you expand in every way.
829	Higher levels of angels are joining your spiritual guide team at this time.
830	Nurture your internal garden. Miracles will bloom and open like flowers around you if you let them.
831	Treat each blessing with respect and reverence, and more will come.
832	When you played small, each challenge kept you that way. As you grow, each challenge keeps you expanding.

833	Be proud of the healing you have done around your ability to receive.
834	Healing is a stage, not a never-ending quest in and of itself.
835	Meditate on how your connection to the Divine aligns with your goals.
836	The angels want you to put in the work on staying positive to fuel the miracles ahead.
837	Taking a chance is a vote of confidence for your future self. Exemplify faith by showing up for what you believe in.
838	You are surrounded by past victories. Notice the goals you have already achieved.
839	Create harmony in your surroundings by being cohesive in how you move through your days.
840	Your higher self is stepping closer to you at this time.
841	Reflect on how your current internal story is playing out in your reality. Rewrite what isn't working, and amplify the positive glimpses you see.
842	Create visible anchors that remind you of your dreams and goals.
843	Love is an action. As you invite in more love, take more actions that open your heart.
844	You are focusing on the end result but need to clear the false narratives that are keeping it from manifesting in your life.
845	Life is messy. Reward yourself for showing up consistently but not perfectly.
846	Identify the limits you put on yourself when it comes to receiving more financial abundance.

847	Each *no* you say to drama and distraction is a *yes* to the Divine's plan for you.
848	You have thrown everything at a situation. Now let it resolve itself.
849	Collapse all timelines by imagining every single dream of yours instantly made real and the kind of person you would be within each dream.
850	People appreciate your help and support more when given freely. Only invest in relationships where there is an equal flow of giving and receiving.
851	Chasing external validation is like fertilizing a fruitless tree. Cultivate contentment through your connection to spirit.
852	You are becoming aware of the most important people in your life at this time.
853	Make a plan of action for setbacks and rejections. You're in charge of your response.
854	Create a daily ritual around grounding, peace, and joy. Invite the angels to join you.
855	You can let go without losing the love that once was. Let every part or party to this situation be free to continue on their own path.
856	Be wholeheartedly yourself, and speak freely and intentionally of what you want to manifest.
857	Go inward and connect to the power of the Divine that beats within your heart.
858	If you are in need of a new adventure, follow your curiosity.
859	Write a gratitude list starting with the tiniest things in your reality first.

860	You need support. Look for new activities, communities, and places to find friends.
861	Add your energy to causes that are aligned with the world you want to be a part of.
862	Notice a negative pattern in your life. Decide on a simple action to redirect it the next time it appears. Ask the angels for help with the follow-through.
863	You're looking at a problem without seeing the solution it presents to a current, bigger predicament. Shift your perspective.
864	Passions can twist into obsessions. Release your grip on things that light you up.
865	To move forward you need to accept the current situation fully.
866	Come back to the tools of reflection that turn up the volume of your own inner voice.
867	Supply sustenance for others by sharing food, shelter, money, or other resources with no expectation of being compensated.
868	The angels have sent you every sign available, and yet you wait for more confirmation. Your desire is the ultimate green light.
869	Talking through your feelings with a loved one will unlock a new understanding. Listen to your own voice.
870	Forgive the people who didn't honor the softness of your heart.
871	Part of your journey is realizing how much you have in common with even your fiercest opponent. Look for similarities and common interests to bridge the gap.

872	Ask for more. You are holding yourself back from receiving in important areas of your life and relationships.
873	Some of your psychic powers lie dormant. Seek out teachers and new ways of activating them.
874	Be honest with yourself and your angels about what truly motivates you. The truth will open up new possibilities.
875	Cultivating positivity is the key to more abundance and joy.
876	You have been replaying old stories in your mind. Extract the lessons instead.
877	You are so much stronger than your biggest fear or failure. Trust your power.
878	Losing faith in others can be part of growing up. Don't let any experience lead to losing faith in yourself.
879	You are in the right place, at the right time, with the right people.
880	You can embody faith even when it's scarce in yourself or others.
881	Dark nights of the soul lead to a deeper appreciation of the light within each new day.
882	To release a painful memory, physical ache, or emotional trauma, you must first accept that it's there; then, let the angels help you let it go.
883	The Universe is a witness to your every triumph and success. You're never celebrating alone.
884	Work on a flaw, weakness, or skill you have held yourself back from exploring.
885	Recommit yourself to speak of and take action on the life you want to build.

886	You're slowing down right before the finish line. Release any doubts and keep going!
887	An attitude of appreciation and positivity will open doors to the rooms you long to be in.
888	Allow yourself to be big and expansive! You are meant to break through patterns that have held back people in your lineage. Enjoy being a chain breaker!
889	So much abundance has passed through your hands already. You're here to impact the direction and energy of money for the greater good of all.
890	New love after loss is the final stage of healing for both souls to move on.
891	As you go through each of your daily rituals and tasks, bless and make holy everything you touch.
892	Your mental state will benefit from time in nature and less energy spent on taking in the words and energy of others.
893	You're letting others' opinions influence deeply personal matters. Listen to your own voice.
894	Let the people who've helped you know the profound impact they've had on your mind, heart, and life.
895	An obstacle is an opportunity to flex your problem-solving skills; you've got this.
896	Show love in the way you know is most impactful for the receiver, even if that is doing something out of the ordinary.
897	You have received good advice and support and are worthy of all the good things coming your way.
898	New versions of you are stepping into proximity. Follow what lights you up.

899	No one succeeds alone; notice how your angels work through all the people in your life.
900	Express gratitude for the past experiences that have led you here today. Each victory and failure was needed in your soul's journey.
901	Reflect on the choices in your past where you followed your intuition and it paid off. You can always rely on your inner voice to steer you.
902	Ask to be met halfway by the Universe, and look for creative compromises.
903	You are not a victim of circumstance. Rewrite the story you're telling yourself.
904	Change can come early or it can come late. No matter how it shows up, it's right on time.
905	Be a reliable custodian of the abundance already in your hands to expand your capacity for prosperity.
906	Your physical body is as sacred and important as your spiritual body. Embrace the needs of both to create more balance in your life.
907	Going deeper in your life will mean letting go of the relationships that only scratch the surface.
908	Ancestral patterns of joy and perseverance are available for you to draw upon.
909	Your root chakra is being worked on. Allow it to deepen your grounding.
910	Act as if what you want is already a fully integrated part of your reality. And so it is.
911	What you are healing right now is needed for the overall expansion of your heart.

912	Decline and reject that which distracts you from your goals. You're so close. Keep going!
913	The Divine Father within is embracing every part of your being, body and soul.
914	Be fluid. Let the angels fill your dance card in life with new experiences and joy.
915	Developing meaningful relationships means you have to allow others to see you on both good and bad days. Embrace imperfection and show up anyway.
916	Your creativity needs a certain level of consistency to flow. Let inspiration find you working.
917	Be an angel to others, and share your lessons, light, and energy.
918	The masculine aspects of your being are being cleared of old assumptions and rejection.
919	Seeking out other viewpoints and perspectives than your own is needed at this time.
920	Identify the limits you put on yourself when it comes to showing up fully.
921	Clarify your values before taking on your next task. Being clear about what you believe in makes each decision part of a larger movement.
922	Say thank you to the people who make your life easier in both mundane and sacred ways.
923	You are deeply connected to the angels that protect and nourish the healers of this world. Trust the energy you feel around you.
924	A romantic relationship needs your attention. Show up for the love you want to last.

925	Personal growth can still become a comparison game with others. There is no competition to beat when it comes to the connection to your higher self.
926	You are being led toward a meeting point for souls that share similar interests and experiences. You are not alone.
927	Remove yourself from spaces where your natural leadership and authority are being ignored or wasted.
928	As you wish to receive at ever-increasing levels, become an expert at giving from an even purer place. Trust that every need you have will be met.
929	Make time for softness and ease after each accomplishment or exertion.
930	What you are healing right now is part of your journey to spiritual mastery.
931	Your ideas can only serve the world by being shared with others. Do not hoard your genius.
932	Create a wave of energy to carry you forward by lightening your load. Let go of the people, places, things, and thoughts that keep you from seeing new parts of the world.
933	Finding and maintaining self-aware friends and positive role models is part of the next stage of your life.
934	What ideas have you abandoned in moments of doubt? Revisit them now.
935	Old hurt can visit us from time to time. Do not allow it to take up precious space in your heart or mind forever.
936	Make a plan for the next unfolding of your path. The angels are paying special attention to you.
937	Ask for direction and it will be given.

938	There are no limits to the love you can receive when you are letting yourself become one with the heart of the Universe.
939	You have proven your worth by simply existing. There are no hoops to jump through.
940	Double the impact of your vision and ideas by sharing them with other lightworkers.
941	Each connection in your life is blessed by the Divine to teach and deliver what is needed right now.
942	There is healing to be done around your relationship with your children and/or inner child.
943	Become a vessel for spiritual love. Let the Divine touch the world through your hands.
944	Be in this moment, and return to the present every time you find yourself lost.
945	Set limits on who has access to your time when your energy is in need of replenishing.
946	You are being seen and appreciated in rooms you have long since left. Never doubt your impact.
947	Pain is part of the admission ticket to expansion. Embrace all the emotions moving through you.
948	Trying to perfect what the Divine has shaped can lead to unhealthy habits. Let yourself appreciate the marvel of your body as it is.
949	You will live many lives in this one and even more before and after it. Embrace the multipassionate path you are walking.
950	Keep asking for exactly what you want and need as clearly as possible.

951	Your friendships are changing; show up for the connections that you want to keep.
952	Be brave in your visions and plans for the future.
953	Your spirituality can transform any mundane task into a sacred one. Infuse your day with intention, and see it become an extended prayer to the Divine.
954	Leading and teaching others is the final stage of integrating and turning a lesson into wisdom.
955	You can embody the light without dimming the brightness of those around you.
956	Practice asking without attachment to the answer or outcome.
957	Your health needs attention: take care of yourself.
958	Spend time envisioning the most challenging parts of your life filled with support and abundance. Anchor yourself in these feelings today.
959	Being fully present with any emotion, especially the hard ones, will expand your capacity for joy and fulfillment.
960	Forgive the people who didn't value your contribution to their life.
961	Your sensitivity is a gift. As you allow your intuition to open, enforce what new boundaries are needed.
962	Create safety in areas where you have let others decide for you before. Safety means you can be soft yet still take action.
963	Shift your perspective to an ever higher one. Everything can be solved from the right vantage point.
964	Move your body, and let any emotion find a channel in your physical exertion.

965	You don't have to understand everything that someone is going through to be there for them.
966	Further investigation is needed. Ask more questions, and get a second or third opinion.
967	Listen to your inner rebel and any counterarguments that are missing from your current conversations.
968	Follow through on your promises even if your situation changes.
969	Help from on high is near. Make sure you can be seen by people ahead of you.
970	Spend equal amounts of time on both the spiritual and practical aspects of your dreams. Each needs the other to fully manifest.
971	Synchronicities are the angels' ways of lighting up your path. Expect to see more signs going forward.
972	Let yourself be supported and comforted by others. Cutting contact with your helpers means the angels will have to get very creative to help you out.
973	The Divine Child within is asking for more playfulness and spontaneity in your days.
974	Any creative endeavor opens your heart to a higher power. Dedicate your art to the Universe.
975	Think of your life and belongings as tools that can support or hinder your connection to your higher self. Release the things that are interfering with that connection.
976	Creating change and going through new experiences can take a toll. Rest, relax, and recharge your batteries.

977	Speaking ill of others, even when warranted by their behavior, is a downward spiral. Detach yourself from gossip and the people who enjoy it.
978	Show appreciation for the gifts that the Universe has given. Appreciation multiplies the gifts coming your way.
979	Align yourself with a state of higher responsibility and leadership.
980	You are a powerful conduit for Divine information. Share your insights with others.
981	Keep reminders and images of your goals and dreams visible around you.
982	You have skills and talents that have been left unexplored. Find ways to reclaim and explore them for no other reason than the joy of it.
983	Pay attention to all the ways your body and mind pick up information from spirit throughout the day.
984	You have survived and learned from every single one of your previous challenges. Acknowledge your endurance, power, and adaptability.
985	Listen to your own voice and the messages you get from your intuition first and foremost. It's time to focus on your own needs.
986	You are worthy of every desire that burns within your heart. Treat yourself accordingly.
987	Ground and connect yourself to the earth, and let the energy of our home in the Universe support you.
988	Identify the limits you put on yourself when it comes to living authentically.

989	Use your body and any physical activity to release what is holding you back.
990	There is so much power in the ending of a chapter. Decide how you want to exit the old and embrace the new.
991	Listen to the voices of possibility. You need to fill your ears and mind with examples of what the Divine has already bestowed on others.
992	Grief, loss, change, and disappointments can weigh heavily on all levels of your being. Let the angels lift it all off your shoulders.
993	Show up for each part of the life you want from the simplest task to advanced manifestation. Flex your spiritual leadership muscles.
994	Put yourself in new contexts and communities. Surround yourself with people who think outside of the box.
995	Notice a positive pattern in your life, and decide on a simple action to amplify its impact. Ask the Universe to support you with it.
996	Be willing to work on your relationship with the Universe. Spend as much time on your spiritual connection as you do on other important relationships in your life.
997	This is a time to fully surrender to faith and let any fear or trepidation dissolve.
998	You can balance all the different parts of you into a coherent whole. There is no need to limit yourself.
999	You have completed a deep cycle of learning and expansion. Rest before the next period of growth and opportunities unfolds.

4

your personal angel numbers

In this chapter, we will go over how to find your personal angel numbers based on the Chaldean numerology system. Personal angel numbers speak to the overall intention and lessons behind your life.

Seeing your personal angel numbers is a reminder to always return to your own authentic expression, focus on the goals that matter most to you, and honor your own inherent power. Never try to twist yourself into something you're not or into being envious of other people's paths and expressions. You are perfect in the eyes of the Divine in this very moment and all that will come after.

Your personal angel numbers are based on the day you were born. You can read through the list of angel numbers and combine all your personal numbers into one long personal message from your guides.

If you were born on the 1st, 10th, 19th, or 28th of any month in any year, your personal angel numbers are 1, 11, 111, 1111, and so on. You might also feel drawn to the numbers that have a digit sum of 1, such as 46, 379, 946, and so forth.

If you were born on the 2nd, 11th, 20th, or 29th of any month in any year, your personal angel numbers are 2, 22, 222, 2222, and so on. You might also feel drawn to the numbers that have a digit sum of 2, such as 47, 551, 884, and so forth.

If you were born on the 3rd, 12th, 21st, or 30th of any month in any year, your personal angel numbers are 3, 33, 333, 333, and so on. You might also feel drawn to the numbers that have a digit sum of 3, such as 39, 606, 813, and so forth.

If you were born on the 4th, 13th, 22nd, or 31st of any month in any year, your personal angel numbers are 4, 44, 444, 4444, and so on. You might also feel drawn to the numbers that have a digit sum of 4, such as 58, 292, 499, and so forth.

If you were born on the 5th, 14th, or 23rd of any month in any year, your personal angel numbers are 5, 55, 555, 5555, and so on. You might also feel drawn to the numbers that have a digit sum of 5, such as 14, 77, 446, and so forth.

If you were born on the 6th, 15th, or 24th of any month in any year, your personal angel numbers are 6, 66, 666, 6666, and so on. You might also feel drawn to the numbers that have a digit sum of 6, such as 24, 87, 996, and so forth.

If you were born on the 7th, 16th, or 25th of any month in any year, your personal angel numbers are 7, 77, 777, 7777, and so on. You might also feel drawn to the numbers that have a digit sum of 7, such as 25, 655, 475, and so forth.

If you were born on the 8th, 17th, or 26th of any month in any year, your personal angel numbers are 8, 88, 888, 8888, and so on. You might also feel drawn to the numbers that have a digit sum of 8, such as 35, 251, 359, and so forth.

If you were born on the 9th, 18th, or 27th of any month in any year, your personal angel numbers are 9, 99, 999, 9999, and so on. You might also feel drawn to the numbers that have a digit sum of 9, such as 36, 522, 909, and so forth.

5

how to deepen your connection to the angels

There is more to you than meets the eye. Huge parts of your energy resources rest in your spiritual self, which wants to connect with a higher power and flow through all aspects of your being. There is an eternal longing within you to merge all levels of your consciousness with the Divine. Deepening your connection to the angels is the work of removing obstacles and examining preconceived ideas and beliefs while eradicating practical stumbling blocks so the lines of communication are clear and unencumbered. The tasks outlined below are deceptively simple, but each one will help clarify and strengthen your connection to the Divine in its own way.

SET THE INTENTION

To deepen your connection to your angels, start by stating your intention to open up all pathways of Divine connection and guidance.

Allow your higher power into all parts of your life from the mundane to the already sacred. If you, while doing this, feel hesitant about including any specific area of your life, make the invitation even more explicit for that area. This could be an extra prayer of intervention, support, and protection for your work, creative pursuits, sexual wellness, physical healing, relationships, and such. The Divine loves a heartfelt invitation, especially in areas where we feel rejected, hold trauma, or think we have thoroughly messed up. Let go and let God do what is needed. Repeat the process of setting the intention as often as you feel inclined to do so. Saying the intention out loud and writing it down gives it extra power.

REMOVE DISTRACTIONS

Our lives are filled with an ever-growing amount of stimulants, interruptions, and redirections combined with a collective attention span that becomes shorter and shorter each year. The Divine lives in every moment but is infinitely more accessible in the quiet spaces and pauses in life. To create an optimal environment for the Divine to join you, start by removing distractions in the form of excess noise, loud notifications, electronics that buzz on your counter, social interactions that drain you, and mindless media consumption. If you have a habit of watching the news or scrolling first thing in the morning, I encourage you to turn off your internet connection and see what having an uninterrupted morning for a week will do for your mental state and bodily awareness. If you are busy, the instinct to speed up, multitask, and be surrounded by more input is normal. The antidote to getting sidetracked and stressed out is to slow down, do one task at a time, and be intentional about the things you allow to fill your days. This extends to the use of stimulants like caffeine, energy drinks, excessively sweet or heavy foods that numb you, or anything consumed in excess that you are using to self-soothe in an unhealthy way.

LIMIT SCREEN TIME

Making space in your days and weeks is beneficial in and of itself. Back when I first moved to the United States, I didn't have a laptop and only used my phone for emails and a little social media. This meant that I would watch movies in the theater, go see plays, get physical copies of books to read instead of scrolling online, and do most things without having a screen in front of me. Coincidentally, my spiritual practice, mental health, creativity, and physical fitness were all flourishing, and the moment a friend lent me a laptop for a project, my priorities shifted and my time automatically became filled with more distractions. While your life and career might require you to sit in front of a screen for hours a day, make sure that your days off have extended periods without access to or the distraction of technology.

YOUR HOME IS A SACRED VISION BOARD

Our physical reality is a mirror of our internal state, and sometimes that inner space is overflowing. This can show up as clutter in our surroundings, holding on to things that remind us of past relationships, and overwhelm in the form of random piles of clothes and papers. It can lead to impulse buys that reflect a fantasy version of ourselves and have no use in our actual lives. Your brain is constantly scanning your surroundings, and if they are filled with messages of scarcity, past regrets, and a never-ending to-do list, then there is no space for the angels to sit. Like your body has a physical elimination process that takes care of what is no longer needed, I encourage you to create a regular process of removing the old and making space and peace for your eyes, so that your surroundings reflect the inner calm and connection you desire. Always start with removing anything that is broken, worn out, or no longer a fit for your current life, body, and goals. If you find that some of your possessions are tied to goals that once were aspirational and now feel commonplace, know it's normal that your desires have changed and leveled up over time.

In the space you free up, there might be a spot for an altar, meditation pillow, or a symbol of the connection you wish to develop with the Divine, like a blooming plant, spiritual imagery, or pictures of ancestors that you feel connected to. The new things you add become physical anchors that represent your goals, dreams, and intentions. These anchors should engage as many of your senses as possible and be in places that you see or move through multiple times a day. Please, only add things after releasing the old, and treat the space as a physical vision board for your life. Apply this approach to smaller spaces too, like your desk or workspace, and make sure there is separation between work, rest, and play spaces.

QUIETING YOUR MIND

While walking around in a continuous meditative state would be wonderful, it would also get in the way of, you know, life. When I talk about quieting your mind, it's not with the end goal of becoming an unflappable Zen master who never gets bothered or worked up. Our objective is to access the higher aspects of your consciousness, the peaceful parts of your being, and the groundedness that comes from spending quality time with the most important person in your life: you. Creating a daily meditation practice of five to ten minutes of quiet contemplation is one of the best ways to set up a regular check-in with the Universe. You can follow guided meditations on YouTube or on free apps. You can listen to meditation music, or just sit in silence and keep guiding your attention back to the breath cycles of your body. It is not the impact of the single session of meditation that is important. It is the willingness to regularly sit in discomfort and wait for whatever wants to come through, again and again, until it becomes an easy and natural habit. If you are new to meditation, you can start by listening to the meditation from the online bonus mentioned on page 109 and then just add an extra five minutes after it to sink a little deeper into yourself.

If you find yourself vehemently opposed to this form of "passive" meditation, then you can pick any mundane physical task and dedicate it to the Divine. This could be vacuuming, doing the dishes, gardening, walking, or such. As your body is engaged with the task, focus your mind on the breath cycles of your body, and allow the thoughts that come up to move through your mind without lingering for long. In this way, you create sacred moments within your daily life that will spill over into the rest of your day and make a boring task have a deeper meaning.

SCHEDULE TIME OFF WITH THE ANGELS

If it's not on your calendar and therefore a nonnegotiable part of your day, then it will not happen. Just as you can schedule time for everything from errands to deep work, you can set aside time for the angels. If it's at the end of the day, then use physical indicators that, over time, help your brain shift its focus automatically to one of reflection and grounding. You can do so by dimming the light, putting your phone on "do not disturb," and incorporating meditation into your wind-down time before bed. If you have the opportunity for it, then set a day, a week, or a month aside for deeper rest and reconnection with your spiritual self.

JOURNALING WITH THE DIVINE

Even if you already journal, there are ways of elevating the practice of putting pen to paper, hands on a keyboard, or notes in a note app. My invitation is to treat your journal sessions as letter writing to the Divine. Try writing a letter to your higher self, the angels, an ancestor, your inner child, all of your maternal line, all of your paternal line, God, the Universe, or a past or future version of yourself. You can use these letter-writing sessions to ask questions and reflect on your experiences, beliefs, and goals. You can pour out old hurt and say all the things you've held back from voicing before. You can write gratitude and appreciation lists to ask the Universe for more of the good stuff. You can keep a running inventory of synchronicities, miracles, compliments from your surroundings, and moments of joy and love in your life.

If your letters become repetitive streams of consciousness, focus on specific things and the present moment or the very near future. Ask the burning questions and for concrete help. Be explicit in your wishes, and always add "I wish for this or something even better" to your requests. Use "I will," "I want," and "I am" statements instead of "I would like," "I should," or "I can't have" statements. Your desires are not dirty and need no justification or qualifiers. As long as your wishes don't hurt anyone else, you should own them wholeheartedly.

Angel Number Journal Prompts

Noticing angel numbers is always an invitation to go deeper and to reflect on the messages from the Divine and how they connect to your current mental, emotional, and physical state. Add structure to your journaling by using the following prompts:

- Angel numbers I've noticed recently:
- When and where did the numbers appear?
- What was going on in my physical, emotional, and spiritual reality at the time?
- What is the meaning behind the numbers according to this book?
- What do I feel is the meaning behind the numbers?
- What action will I take based on these messages?
- What other signs and intuitive hits do I connect to this experience?
- If my understanding of the numbers has changed over time, what new aspect do I now see?
- Further reflections:

ELEVATING YOUR CURRENT RITUALS AND PRACTICES

You might have a solid lifelong meditation habit, live a minimalist and distraction-free life with a maximalist spiritual practice, and yet feel like there is something missing. Maybe you have become rigid in your approach to the Divine? Then you need to engage deeper with all of your senses and let some playfulness in. We all get stuck in restrictive approaches when it comes to our spiritual connection and creative expansion. But relying on one mode of communication with the Divine is like limiting yourself to using only one of your senses to experience life.

Think about how you could elevate your current practice. It could be through looking for new meditation music or creating playlists that complement the energy you want to surround yourself with. You could hang windchimes or do sound baths. Use candles, incense, essential oils, or fresh flowers to infuse your space and nose with new scents. You could refresh the imagery in your home; bring more life inside through plants, crystals, and water features; or take the whole practice outside in nature. If you feel isolated, you could expand your solo practice into a community by attending meditation circles online or in person. If none are available near you, you could start your own and invite others. Traveling to spiritual spaces like Bali, Glastonbury, Bhutan, Egypt, and such could give you access to the particular energy of those places and invigorate your own. Going on any kind of spiritual retreat is a great way to level up your practice through immersion and being around people with the same desire for depth as you. Signing up for a course or training within a new field or with a new teacher is yet another way to level up and expand your practice.

SACRED MOVEMENT

As mentioned before, you can devote any mundane physical task to the Divine and use it as a form of active meditation. If bringing your body further into your spiritual practice feels good, then you can seek out sacred movement practices like Osho Active Meditations, ecstatic dance, 5Rhythms, Kundalini yoga, tai chi, and breathwork. You can devote self-pleasure sessions to the Divine, and if your partner is open, then any sensual and sexual practice can be amplified by sharing a few moments of meditation before any physical touch. This could lead to exploring tantric meditations or practices together. If you have trauma around your sensual, sexual, and creative expression, make sure to only move forward with sacred movement at the pace your body is comfortable with. As author Peta Kelly writes, *You go first, the Universe goes further.*

TRUST THAT YOU'RE BEING MET HALFWAY

Going deeper with any aspect of the Divine is a process of allowing yourself to slow down, focus on even the tiniest detail, and get fully lost in the expression of God that's present in each moment of your life. The access point could be through smells, tastes, feelings, or physical sensations. The communication could be as subtle as shifts in light, color, temperature, pressure, or sound, anything that you move through that heightens or lessens in intensity as you focus on it.

Let yourself be met where you are in this moment. Follow the nudges and intuitive hits that come through as you slow down. If part of your desire is to meet or create something new, please know that who and what you're looking for is already on its way and reaching out to you too.

I highly recommend that you journal on the different ways you feel the presence of the Divine already. As you focus on the familiar visits from the angels, you will start noticing even more moments of connection. It could be through physical sensations such as getting goosebumps or feeling a light wind or touch. Notice feathers, rainbows, butterflies, birds, cloud patterns, coins, bees, or any animal that feels significant. You could also get visits from the angels when you sleep and through daydreams.

6

what if i stop seeing angel numbers?

Seeing angel numbers can come in waves, depending on our level of openness, where we are on our spiritual journey, and if we need support during a season of change in our lives. When we start seeing them, we get excited, and our primary feelings are often joy, curiosity, and comfort. However, over time, we might start relying on different tools, and our attention might drift beyond the numbers. Where they were a primary sign in the beginning, they become less of a focus.

As humans, we have a tendency to look for complexity. If something is too easy, immediate, and quick, we can come to discount it. The conditioning of most of our societies leads to a mentality that only the things we work hard for have any value. This extends to our spirituality, and so the easier we connect, the more we have a habit of sabotaging the process as we look for challenges and not for open doors. Angel numbers are signposts and confirmation from our spirit team, not something that needs hours of deciphering or mental work. If you have stopped seeing angel numbers and are concerned, try releasing the need for control and focusing on connecting inward, grounding yourself, and letting the messages show up in other ways for a while.

THE END OF A CYCLE

What we rely on at the beginning of our spiritual journey is not always the same tool we use toward the middle or as part of a more professional mastery of our intuitive gifts. Seeing angel numbers is often a precursor to an opening toward other spiritual fields, whether it be the deeper study of numerology, the practice of meditation, or Reiki initiation; or the exploration of systems like astrology or human design; or even more somatic tools like yoga, tai chi, and breathwork. If the experience of not seeing angel numbers occurs during a period of your life that has to do with a redirection of your focus or a sense of graduation, then gratitude is the key that unlocks the next level of working with the numbers.

LET GO OF THE PAST

When we open our intuition, we often allow more nature-based and cyclical living into our days. Working with the numbers will lead you to recognize the cycles of life, and if you're in the quiet of winter energetically, it makes sense that there is less activity in your auric field. This is part of the process. You can meditate on the energy of the number 9 to see if there are some lessons around endings that need to be integrated and honored before a new cycle begins and angel numbers begin to pop up again.

BECOMING PROACTIVE IN YOUR SPIRITUAL ENDEAVORS

You could have interacted with the numbers in a reactive way before this point, and the current quiet is an invitation to be more proactive in your spiritual evolution. What would it feel like to set intentions and take action without waiting for the signs? Do you have fears about missing out, or are you easily swayed by outside influence? The lesson here is that you can rely on yourself and know that your angels are always working for your greatest good, even when you don't hear from them for a while.

CREATING A BLIND SPOT

If you have been ignoring the angels and the messages repeatedly even though they still show up, you could have created a blind spot around them. Instead of focusing on what the signs mean or why you can't see them, just relax and redirect your attention to what blocks you could work on around receiving and what is possibly standing in the way of the message.

AN INTENTIONAL PAUSE

The angels could be regrouping; they might try again later, use a different medium, or talk through the people around you. They could be giving you a break so you can focus on a specific task that will take all your attention for a while.

WHEN YOU ASK FOR THE ANGELS TO STOP TALKING

If your doubt and fear of connecting deeper or following the information you get to the end are overwhelming, then the angels will do the most loving thing and refrain from continuing to send you messages that make you afraid.

RETURN TO THE PRESENT MOMENT

Your need for support is always evolving, and while a lot of angel number sightings can be fun, they can also become a crutch that makes your eyes gloss over other important aspects of your life and surroundings. Having tunnel vision around angel numbers is like being in your car with a friend and driving down a pretty street with your windows down as the seasons change from winter to spring. Instead of marveling at the beautiful scenery, enjoying the easy companionship, and breathing in the fresh spring air while letting the sun warm your skin, you're instead constantly glancing at the GPS wondering if you're going in the right direction. If we get too stuck on making sure that we're on the right path, we could miss the whole purpose of being alive and present in our lives. The point of our journey on earth isn't the destination, but the experience and transformation. It's who you become on the way. Return to the present moment, and know that the ride you're on is the right one.

7

frequently asked questions

Q: What if I see numbers beyond the ones in this book?
A: If you see longer sequences, try breaking them down into the pairings that stand out to you; then look at the different messages behind them. If any one number is repeated more often within the sequence, look at the general meaning behind it.

Q: What does it mean when a number is repeated, like 1212?
A: Repeating compound numbers are like steps on a ladder. Seeing them means that you are integrating the current lesson and getting ready to take a step up the ladder to a new one.

Q: I'm seeing a lot of mirrored numbers like 15:51. What do they mean?

A: Mirrored numbers indicate that your reflection and attention are needed. Don't move on until you have looked at the situation from multiple viewpoints. You could be missing out on a detail, lesson, or connection.

Q: Is there a reason I see single numbers, or patterns of two, three, or four angel numbers more often than others?

A: Most people will see one number sequence first. 11:11 is a common initiator, and seeing your birthdate is another one. As you get more familiar with the numbers and as your connection to your angels grows, you might develop a sense of the numbers building up to a crescendo, going dormant for a while, then reappearing in new sequences. As the numbers are a conversation between you and the angels, there will be many repeat messages. Based on your actions and thoughts about your life, they will evolve or stay the same.

Q: I've been seeing the numbers of my birthdate and/or time of birth. What does that mean?

A: There are many ways to read the map of a soul. If you keep being referred back to the numbers of your birthdate or birth time, then working with a numerologist, astrologer, or human design reader could help you see what kind of energy you are here to explore. There is something in the portal of your birth that you have yet to discover or part of your path you're shying away from.

Q: I don't see any new numbers, just the same numbers over and over again. They never change, and I've seen them for years. What does that mean?

A: One of the fundamental laws in numerology states that the more times a number appears, the stronger the energy, vibration, and message behind it becomes. If the message is constant and you have already acted on it, then you might be called to study numerology or another spiritual tool in depth to cultivate your intuition and strengthen your spiritual connection. Seeing the same numbers all the time, on top of a feeling of frustration or stagnation, is a sign that there is an exit on the road you're traveling that you keep ignoring. Exploring the spiritual aspects of your being can feel like a detour from your normal life, but it is in fact a path to feeling more related to the world and embracing your place and part in it.

Q: Why is the message not clear? Why can't my angels and guides just give me a straightforward answer?

A: The messages from our guides are usually clear and concise the moment they arrive, but our brain jumps into action immediately, starting to categorize the information, and comparing it to what we already know about a situation. Then our emotions start flooding in and muddying the waters further. If our actions and thoughts are a bit all over the place and we lack focus, the angel numbers can reflect this scattered energy as well.

Listening to the spiritual guidance available often means we have to peel back some of our conditioning and expectations around communication. The channel inside of you that the Divine occupies is right next to your childhood's unbridled imagination and creativity. If you have taught yourself to shut down your playfulness, then opening up to your higher power will also be a journey of coaxing your inner child to come out to play too.

Q: I used to see a lot of repeating numbers, such as 333 or 222. Then I started to see a lot of 1222, 1234, 818, and so forth. Now I notice longer and longer sequences! What does this mean?

A: If we look at learning angel numbers in the same way we look at learning a new language, then seeing repeating numbers is like picking up on the general sounds. Once those are established in your mind, you'll start catching more nuances of the structure as your vocabulary expands, and the functions and context of the language become clear. Even if your fluency in deciphering angel numbers seems to stay the same, seeing new complex sequences could reflect your general growing spiritual awareness.

Q: My understanding of the angel numbers has shifted over time. I'm not sure if I should rely on the description I read or the sense I have of them now?

A: Your own intuitive understanding and connection are always the right ones. Angel numbers and their descriptions are always an invitation for further spiritual exploration and connection. Each number describes an aspect of the spectrum of energy available to us. As you grow, your understanding of the numbers will change, and you might move up or down that spectrum of energy as well.

Q: I was brought up within organized religion. This kind of spiritual exploration was heavily discouraged. I'm having a hard time accepting angel numbers as messages from God. Can angel numbers be used by negative or malicious forces?

A: If we allow fear in, focus on the negative, give in to old doubts, or have been shamed or ridiculed for our spirituality or way of understanding our higher power, then any messages we receive can be tainted by that energy. If on top of this, a very narrow understanding of God was described, constantly regulated, and enforced by outside authorities, then your starting point is untangling the messages and unlearning what no longer fits your life and spiritual call.

Before engaging further with angel numbers, it would be beneficial to take inventory of your core spiritual beliefs. See if any underlying story of being broken, corrupted, or a sinner in the eyes of society or God is directing your thoughts. If you have a history of ignoring or violating your internal ethical and moral compass, some forgiveness work could be in order. If you feel like you are not worthy of Divine love, attention, and guidance, the idea that a negative force is influencing you can take root. Return to the numbers when you're ready.

REFERENCES

Gray, K. *Angel Numbers.* Carlsbad, CA: Hay House, 2022.

Hopler, W. "Guardian Angels in Hinduism." Learn Religions, August 26, 2020. www.learnreligions.com/guardian-angels-in -hinduism-124346.

Michaela, M. *The Angel Numbers Book.* New York: Simon and Schuster, 2021.

Virtue, D., and Lynnette Brown. *Angel Numbers.* Carlsbad, CA: Hay House, 2005.

Wilder, N. *A Little Bit of Numerology.* New York: Sterling Publishing, 2019.

ANGEL NUMBERS MEDITATION

You have reached the end of the book! I hope you have enjoyed learning more about angel numbers and how to work with them. Remember that you can use this book as a quick reference tool when you spot an angel number and the journal prompts to track your understanding of them.

If you would like some extra support on your journey, I've created a free meditation to deepen your connection and sharpen your focus when communicating with the angels. You can download and listen to it whenever you need to ground, align, and connect with your higher power.

The Angel Numbers Playlist was my soundscape as I wrote this book, and it's a perfect accompaniment to your reading and can be used as meditation music for the future.

You can find both right here: www.novaleewilder.com/angel-bonus.

ACKNOWLEDGMENTS

Getting to write books will never get old to me, and I'm grateful for each and every person who reads them. Whether you are a new reader or have picked this one up because you enjoyed *A Little Bit of Numerology*, I'm so happy that I get to share my love of the spiritual world of numbers with you.

My thanks go out to all the readers who've reached out with questions and aha moments from their own life, and who were so kind to leave reviews after reading. For the people who became clients and students, I'm so proud to be able to share my passion for numerology with such curious and courageous souls. For everyone who listened to a podcast or read an article I was featured in and then reached out, I love connecting with you and the comments and stories you send me; keep them coming!

For this book, I owe special thanks to my friend and mentor Maria Saraphina, who, with her loving frankness, reminded me that I should write my ideas down and make them real instead of talking them to death. The time between inspiration and action will hopefully only get shorter going forward.

I want to thank the brilliant Mara Marchesi for our bi-weekly talks about everything going on in our worlds from Los Angeles to Italy and London. You have kept me sane since 2020, and I'm so grateful for our friendship.

My biggest thanks always goes to my husband, whose love makes me believe that everything will be okay as long as we do it together. I also have to thank our cat Tikru for being the best procrastination partner a writer could find.

Finally, I want to thank my editor, Kate Zimmermann, who was so open to working on this book and to have me share more numerology nerdiness with the world.

ABOUT THE AUTHOR

Novalee Wilder is a Danish actress and artist turned professional numerologist and writer. She was introduced to numerology through her own name change in 2014, and its effect on all levels of her life ignited a passion for studying this esoteric science. She is now an expert in the field and specializes in name changes.

Novalee lives in sunny Los Angeles with her husband. When she is not teaching, writing, sharing, or thinking about numerology, she is cuddling her cat Tikru and going for long walks.

Novalee has been featured as a numerology expert in Well+Good, *Today*, *USA Today*, Bustle, Thrive Global, *Woman's Day*, and numerous podcasts. She is the author of *A Little Bit of Numerology* and *A Little Bit of Angel Numbers*, host of *The Numerology Podcast* and founder of The Numerology School. She offers name change sessions for all ages, mentorship, training, and talks about the sacred spiritual science of numbers and letters. Learn more at www.novaleewilder.com.

INDEX